COME UP
HERE

COME UP HERE

HERE

Jesus the Warrior King Is Coming Soon

Mark Nyarko

Library of Congress Control Number:		2018905265
ISBN:	Hardcover	978-1-5434-9003-9
	Softcover	978-1-5434-9004-6
	eBook	978-1-5434-9005-3

Scripture quotations marked NKJV are taken from the New King James Version. Copyright © 1982 by Thomas Nelson, Inc. Used by permission. All rights reserved.

Scripture quotations marked NIV are taken from the Holy Bible, New International Version®. NIV®. Copyright © 1973, 1978, 1984 by International Bible Society. Used by permission of Zondervan. All rights reserved. [Biblica]

Any people depicted in stock imagery provided by Getty Images are models, and such images are being used for illustrative purposes only.
Certain stock imagery © Getty Images.

Print information available on the last page.

Rev. date: 05/02/2018

To order additional copies of this book, contact:
Xlibris
800-056-3182
www.Xlibrispublishing.co.uk
Orders@Xlibrispublishing.co.uk
776607

CONTENTS

INTRODUCTION TO THE BOOK OF REVELATION

Every good author leaves the climax of his/her story till the very last chapter. The reader must be held in suspense and anticipation till the last chapter. That is where the reader is to discover how the story ends, how the key questions are answered, what finally happens to the main characters, and how the mystery is finally resolved. If the above observation is true and anybody who has read a bit will agree that it is the case, then the book of Revelation—God's final chapter in the unfolding drama of the ages in His redemptive programme for mankind—should be the most thrilling finale of all the great episodes in the redemption story.

It is therefore heartbreaking that many of God's children have an aversion for this capstone of divine literature because the devil has done such a good work in convincing them it is the one book they cannot expect to read and understand. How sad.

God is the greatest storyteller of all time, and He has left His very best news (for His children) in the very last book. As its name implies, it is the one book above all else where what was hitherto hidden has been revealed, uncovered, made plain and visible. For one to really understand God's great, spellbinding redemption story for His creation in general and mankind in particular, one needs a good understanding of this crowning jewel of books. In the same way, the author will introduce His plot, set the entire storyline, establish His main characters, and set the stage for the entire drama in the very introductory chapter(s). One equally needs a good background understanding of the book of Genesis, which sets the stage for the entire story.

In the same way, for one to really make any sense of what is happening in our day, which is generally agreed to be the very end of times in which we are keenly anticipating the return of Christ to earth, it is equally important for the believer in Christ to understand the book of Daniel, which gives a broad, long-range telescopic view of events from Daniel's day to the very times in which we live. The book of Daniel provides an amazingly accurate political framework of a video or panoramic commentary of history from Daniel's day to the very end times, up to and including the Second Coming of Christ to establish His millennial kingdom on earth. The book of Revelation fills in the broad outline of Daniel with detailed accounts of events, especially those leading to the end of the current dispensation of grace and the period immediately following.

For example, when we read in Galatians 3:13–14 that 'Christ has redeemed us from the curse of the law . . . that the blessing of Abraham might come upon the gentiles in Christ Jesus', this is nice, but it is a strange language to the New Testament believer who may not understand the blessing of Abraham beyond the fact that he was rich and what the curse of the law really was!

Without a good understanding of these Old Testament concepts, appropriating the blessing of Abraham becomes a hollow pursuit. Before we can fully appropriate the lofty blessings of New Covenant grace in Christ, most of which have their roots in the Old Testament, we need a good understanding of who the Jews are, their origins as a distinct group of people, and God's dealings with them in their history. What exactly is the curse of the law, and how does it manifest in one's life? How does Christ's redemptive work on the cross free us from the curse of the law and make us children of Abraham? What exactly is included in the blessing of Abraham, and how do we appropriate these?

As a New Covenant preacher of grace, I firmly believe that the wisdom behind the Old Testament law was from God and hence eternal. Can one imagine for a moment that the imperative to love God and neighbour are no longer valid to a New Covenant believer, that the morality stipulated by the law are no longer relevant because of grace, that the lofty place of family and society, marriage and children are no longer valid?

Look at the devastation of families, communities, and societies in general all around us today. As enlightened modern people, we pride ourselves with deeper spiritual insight into God's Word and soul-stirring expository preaching from coast to coast. It is because modern man has taken his eyes off the building blocks of life and communities and societies in general, which is God's blueprint for life as enshrined in His law. It was this law—which became the bedrock of Jewish social, community, and family life—that caused them to prosper more than any other group of people both in antiquity and today. They are life preserving because they came from the mind and wisdom of God. If anything, we need to pay greater attention to our diet and hygiene in today's complex societies than was ever required in Old Testament days; only we may not do these legalistically.

Yes, the Old Testament laws may look harsh and unreasonable to the casual observer, but they resulted in the well-structured communities and societies in which law and order prevailed, children had both parents growing up, there was respect for marriage and family, sexual and moral restraint was the encouraged and even mandated, respect for elders and parents was the norm, and excellence in industry and agriculture was the norm in Jewish societies.

In the same way, Revelation answers pertinent questions that would otherwise go unanswered: Will sin continue forever? What about the sorrow and pain and the obvious injustices of today's world? What about criminals that evade capture or justice? What about corrupt practices that have blighted nations and multitudes but the perpetrators were either too powerful to face justice or simply got away with their crimes? Will the church be raptured and when, in relation to the tribulation and the Second Coming of the Lord? What is the order of events in the end times and the tribulation? What is Daniel's seventieth week and the tribulation? Who is the Antichrist, and where will he come from? When will Armageddon be fought and by whom? What is the ultimate end of the devil and evildoers? What will happen to the present heaven and earth? When will the new heaven and the new earth come? And as a believer, what rational position should you take in relation to all these seemingly intractable questions?

All these and many other relevant questions are answered by the Revelation. Is it any wonder the devil has kept many believers from this crucial book for millennia? Of course, he does not want you to know the miserable end of his ignominious, rebellious career. Of course, he does not want you to know how Genesis 3:14–15 prophecy pronounced by the Lord on him is finally fulfilled in Revelation 20:1–3, 10.

> So the LORD God said to the serpent:
> 'Because you have done this,
> You *are* cursed more than all cattle,
> And more than every beast of the field;
> On your belly you shall go,
> And you shall eat dust
> All the days of your life.
> And I will put enmity
> Between you and the woman,
> And between your seed and her Seed;
> He shall bruise your head,
> And you shall bruise His heel.'
> (Genesis 3:14–15)

> Then I saw an angel coming down from heaven, having the key to the bottomless pit and a great chain in his hand. He laid hold of the dragon, that serpent of old, who is the Devil and Satan, and bound him for a thousand years; and he cast him into the bottomless pit, and shut him up, and set a seal on him, so that he should deceive the nations no more till the thousand years were finished. But after these things he must be released for a little while.

> The devil, who deceived them, was cast into the lake of fire and brimstone where the beast and the false prophet

are. And they will be tormented day and night forever and ever.

(Revelation 20:1–3, 10)

Then from Genesis 3:14–15, we come to John 8:44, Luke 10:17–19, Mark 16:17–18, Acts 26:17–18, Revelation 12:7–9, and finally, Revelation 20:1–3, 10, when he is no more. He does not want you to see his miserable end. But Revelation lays it all bare in the open. It shows the imminence of the Lord's return, that the tribulation is not forever, and that heaven is a place not to be missed for anything. All these give hope to the believer to carry on in the face of daunting trials and ridicule and an incentive to run and finish the race for the prize laid up for us. All these are clearly made clear in the Revelation.

Even more reassuring is the fact that in our day, the Lord has opened up hitherto hidden mysteries and afforded us greater understanding as these are the times we need these truths to guide us as we come closer and closer to the end of time, the end of the age.

In Daniel, He tells the prophet:

> And the vision of the evenings and mornings which was told is true; Therefore seal up the vision, For it refers to many days in the future.
>
> (Daniel 8:26)

> But you, Daniel, shut up the words, and seal the book until the time of the end; many shall run to and fro, and knowledge shall increase.
>
> (Daniel 12:4)

> And he said, 'Go your way, Daniel, for the words are closed up and sealed till the time of the end.'
>
> (Daniel 12:9)

In all the above scriptures, the Lord is clearly saying that these great prophecies may not necessarily be understood by earlier generations but

He will make them clearly to the generation of the times of the end to whom it would be even more relevant. This is what is happening in our day. The Lord is making His Word more and more clear to us as we need the great truths expounded in them to guide our lives and profession in the days in which we live, where our major focus should be on getting ourselves and others ready for His soon return. This is true of all scripture but more so with the prophetic word about the end times, which has come upon us.

> Many shall be purified, made white, and refined, but
> the wicked shall do wickedly; and none of the wicked
> shall understand, but the wise shall understand.
>
> (Daniel 12:10)

How true it is that as the world gets more wicked and darker, the peoples thereof do not have a clue what is about to descend on this world. They won't even believe it even if you told them. It will be met with certain ridicule. But the children of light, who are walking with their Lord, all understand what the world is heading for, and are getting themselves ready for His imminent appearance. This is the major theme of 1 Thessalonians 5:1–11 as I have expounded elsewhere in this book.

So Revelation is crucial in answering many of the puzzles in the scriptures and giving the necessary encouragement and motivation to all Christians and more so to the weary soldier who is often tempted to be discouraged, slow down, or even give up altogether. It is a clarion call to the weary soul that help is on the way and very soon.

Keep on believing because your redemption draws nigh. Supper is ready, and the bridegroom is on the way. When the bridegroom appears, the waiting is over. There would be no need for fasting any more as we switch to party mode. Weary soldier, be encouraged. The finish line is in sight. We near the footsteps outside the door. The galloping of heaven's horses and the advance winds of His refreshing presence are beginning to blow.

KEYS TO INTERPRET BIBLE PROPHECY

There are simple but precise guidelines for interpreting the Word of God in general and the prophetic scriptures in particular, which, if carefully followed, would always let one know the intended message by God. We should be careful not to impute our own human understanding and interpretation to God's Word. as the Apostle Peter wisely advised in 1 Peter 1:20–21, 'Knowing this first, that no prophecy of scripture is of any private interpretation, for prophecy never came by the will of man, but holy men of God spoke as they were moved by the Holy Spirit.'

In fact, God gives a stern warning with severe sanctions in Revelation 22:18–19 for us to not add to or take away from His Word. Let the text speak for itself. It is very important to have a totally settled mind about the authenticity of the totality of the scriptures for a start. Once one begins to allow any shade of doubt about any aspect or portion of the Word, you will undermine your faith completely and will not be sure about any aspect of it, and you will begin to cherry-pick what to believe and what not to believe.

Hebrews 11:6 declares:

> But without faith *it is* impossible **to** please *Him,* for **he who comes to God must believe that He is**, and *that* **He is** a rewarder of those **who** diligently seek Him.

What is true of God is even more true of His Word because God's Word is His bond. According to Hebrews 6:17–18:

Thus God, determining to show more abundantly to the heirs of promise the immutability of His counsel, confirmed *it* by an oath, that by two immutable things, in which it *is* impossible for God to lie, we might have strong consolation, who have fled for refuge to lay hold of the hope set before *us*.

The scripture is saying God cannot lie. The entire Bible, from Genesis to Revelation, is a statement of truth or is truthfully stated. In addition, God has sworn by Himself to reinforce the unchangeableness or immutability of His Word. So not only do we have His Word, we have His oath to back His Word, as if to say, 'You can trust Me and My Word under any and every circumstance or situation.'

In addition, understand that there is zero chance of the scriptures being falsified in any way. At the time of writing most of the New Testament, which was generally within a few decades of Christ's death and resurrection, the Old Testament, the Jewish Torah, had been closed for over four hundred silent years after the ministry of the prophet Malachi, during which time God ceased talking to His people through the prophets. Also, the Jews were generally hostile to the new religion, which they regarded as a cult, and they did everything to kill it at birth. The apostles and the gospel writers often alluded to eyewitness accounts, to which their audiences must have been complicit, to make their point, but none of the hearers could contradict what they said and wrote.

For instance, Peter said on the day of Pentecost:

Men of Israel, hear these words: Jesus of Nazareth, a Man attested by God to you by miracles, wonders, and signs which God did through Him in your midst, as you yourselves also know—Him, being delivered by the determined purpose and foreknowledge of God, you have taken by lawless hands, have crucified, and put to death; whom God raised up, having loosed the pains of death, because it was not possible that He should be held by it.

(Acts 2:22–24)

'Therefore let all the house of Israel know assuredly that God has made this Jesus, whom you crucified, both Lord and Christ.'

(Acts 2:36)

But you denied the Holy One and the Just, and asked for a murderer to be granted to you, and killed the Prince of life, whom God raised from the dead, of which we are witnesses.

(Acts 3:14–15)

Yet now, brethren, I know that you did *it* in ignorance, as *did* also your rulers.

(Acts 3:17)

In 2 Peter 1:16–21, Peter appealed to his readers to trust the prophetic word, because he saw and experienced the very things he was writing about. He was saying that these were not man-made stories concocted by someone's fertile imagination but that the very source of the Word was God the Spirit Himself, who got men to write what He wanted written. Hence, you can fully trust the Word, and anyone who heeds the Word will have the inner confirmation within their own hearts. He is saying you can prove the source and veracity of the Word by paying heed and meditating on it. The Word is self-authenticating.

For we did not follow cunningly devised fables when we made known to you the power and coming of our Lord Jesus Christ, but were eyewitnesses of His majesty. For He received from God the Father honor and glory when such a voice came to Him from the Excellent Glory: 'This is My beloved Son, in whom I am well pleased.'

And we heard this voice which came from heaven when we were with Him on the holy mountain.

And so we have the prophetic word confirmed, which you do well to heed as a light that shines in a dark place, until the day dawns and the morning star rises in your hearts; knowing this first, that no prophecy of Scripture is of any private interpretation, for prophecy never came by the will of man, but holy men of God spoke *as they were* moved by the Holy Spirit.

(2 Peter 1:16–21)

Peter is inviting his readers to prove the truth of the Word themselves by paying heed to it.

Paul also made a direct allusion in his great gospel pitch to eyewitness accounts before his hearers in 1 Corinthians 15:3–8 when he wrote:

For I delivered to you first of all that which I also received: that Christ died for our sins according to the Scriptures, and that He was buried, and that He rose again the third day according to the Scriptures, and that He was seen by Cephas, then by the twelve. After that He was seen by over five hundred brethren at once, of whom the greater part remain to the present, but some have fallen asleep. After that He was seen by James, then by all the apostles. Then last of all He was seen by me also, as by one born out of due time.

In all these, what the apostles are saying is that you are all eyewitnesses to what we are talking about. It all happened before your eyes; these are not fairy tales but something you all saw and experienced. Now, you can only make such a bold assertion if you know that what you are saying is the truth, nothing but the whole truth. The Jews did everything they could to stop them, such as intimidating, flogging, and imprisoning them and forbidding them to speak in the name of Jesus, but the one thing they could not accuse them of was lying or fabrication.

When Paul appeared before King Agrippa (in Acts 26) in his defence of the gospel, he had this to say to the king:

> For the king, before whom I also speak freely, knows these things; for I am convinced that none of these things escapes his attention, since this thing was not done in a corner.
>
> (Acts 26:26)

In effect, Paul was saying to the king, 'You know about what I am talking about, because it is public knowledge.' If anyone knew Jesus and the events of His life and ministry, surely the apostle John should. He was the apostle who prided himself as the one whom Jesus loved and always lay in His bosom. Is it any wonder for him to begin his epistle with these words of intimacy?

What Was Heard, Seen, and Touched

> That which was from the beginning, which we have heard, which we have seen with our eyes, which we have looked upon, and our hands have handled, concerning the Word of life—the life was manifested, and we have seen, and bear witness, and declare to you that eternal life which was with the Father and was manifested to us—that which we have seen and heard we declare to you, that you also may have fellowship with us; and truly our fellowship *is* with the Father and with His Son Jesus Christ.
>
> (1 John 1:1–3)

Luke, the physician, not an apostle himself but one closely associated with those that travelled with Jesus, has these reassuring opening words to the gospel that bears his name:

> Inasmuch as many have taken in hand to set in order a narrative of those things which have been fulfilled among us, just as those who from the beginning were eyewitnesses and ministers of the word delivered them to us, it seemed good to me also, having had perfect understanding of all things from the very first, to write to you an orderly account, most excellent Theophilus, that you may know the certainty of those things in which you were instructed.
>
> (Luke 1:1–4)

What were the opponents' and the Jewish hierarchy's responses to all these? Listen to their own testimony in Acts 4:13–22:

> Now when they saw the boldness of Peter and John, and perceived that they were uneducated and untrained men, they marveled. And they realized that they had been with Jesus. And seeing the man who had been healed standing with them, they could say nothing against it. But when they had commanded them to go aside out of the council, they conferred among themselves, saying, 'What shall we do to these men? For, indeed, that a notable miracle has been done through them *is* evident to all who dwell in Jerusalem, and we cannot deny *it*. But so that it spreads no further among the people, let us severely threaten them, that from now on they speak to no man in this name.'

> So they called them and commanded them not to speak at all nor teach in the name of Jesus. But Peter and

John answered and said to them, 'Whether it is right in the sight of God to listen to you more than to God, you judge. For we cannot but speak the things which we have seen and heard.' So when they had further threatened them, they let them go, finding no way of punishing them, because of the people, since they all glorified God for what had been done. For the man was over forty years old on whom this miracle of healing had been performed.

What all the religious hierarchy could do was to threaten and intimidate them even though they had the power to proscribe and possibly kill off this embryonic movement in its crib. Perhaps they lacked the moral courage to do so, knowing they were acting against their own consciences.

What all these gospel writers are saying is that the scriptures are reliable and true; we were there when it all happened, as were many of you. Now if there was any effort on anybody's part to stretch any of the facts, this would have backfired spectacularly as the Jews would have seized on that quickly to discredit the whole young movement and killed it in the womb before it even got started. They could not disprove any of the claims the apostles made because these were all true and the common people knew it to be so. They could not disprove the gospel, they could not disprove the resurrection of Jesus, and they certainly could not disprove the miracles. More importantly, the New Testament complemented and completed the Old Testament in a way that only the finger of God could guarantee.

Remember that, like the Old Testament, the New Testament was written by different authors at different times in different locations, often in different continents, but when their writings were brought together, there was a perfect fit from beginning to finish. You can totally rely on the scriptures as God's infallible Word to man.

Besides, when you do as it says you should, you will certainly receive the result it promises. If you call the name of Jesus for salvation, you sure get saved. If you call the name for healing, you sure get healed. If you call it for deliverance, you sure get delivered. One big proof of the source of the Word is that it works. His Word is backed by His oath of promise.

> Thus God, determining to show more abundantly to the heirs of promise the immutability of His counsel, confirmed *it* by an oath, [18]that by two immutable things, in which it *is* impossible for God to lie, we might have strong consolation, who have fled for refuge to lay hold of the hope set before *us*.
>
> (Hebrews 6:17–18)

A Warning

For I testify to everyone who hears the words of the prophecy of this book: If anyone adds to these things, God will add to him the plagues that are written in this book; and if anyone takes away from the words of the book of this prophecy, God shall take away his part from the Book of Life, from the holy city, and *from* the things which are written in this book.

This is the cause of much of the confusion in the body today. People are putting their human understanding on the Word instead of seeking the mind of God about what He meant by what He wrote. The Holy Spirit should be the start to finish of all Bible study. He is the author, and only He knows and understands what He wrote.

James (3:1) cautions us not take the burden of teaching God's Word upon ourselves as teachers would receive a stricter judgement.

If one had the option, we would rather do anything else but presume to teach His Word. But having said that, there are clear guidelines to follow, and with the help of the Holy Spirit, we can do all things through the Anointed One and His Anointing, which strengthens us. God sent us His Word for us to read, understand, and apply to our lives (Revelation 1:3) so we do not have to imagine that we need some special intelligence/education to understand the Word. Yes, we must always read and study the Word prayerfully, with the help of the Holy Spirit, the divine author Himself. The greatest barrier to knowledge, it has been said, is to assume that you already know.

1. Give the same meaning to the words of prophecy as you would to the words of history or any other literature. Words mean the same in the Bible as they mean outside the Bible. It is not true that words assume mystical meanings, different from what they would normally mean in ordinary usage. For example, a year in the Bible is not a day, and a day is not a year. A year is a year, and a day is a day. God knows what a year means and what a day is. This unwarranted substitution has been the cause of much confusion. For example, *day* and *night* in Genesis 1 mean exactly that—not centuries, not seasons, not millennia, but the literal twenty-four-hour days as are the associated evenings and mornings.

2. Do not change the literal to a spiritual or symbolic meaning. For example, *earthquakes, trumpets, grass* all mean the same in the Bible as outside it. If a symbol is used to represent the real thing, look for the meaning in the Word itself, often in the immediate context. This assumes that God intended His revelation to be understood by all who believe because His communication is based on the regular laws of written communication. *Literal sense* means the usual, customary, socially accepted meaning conveyed by words and expressions in their usual contexts. The literal sense does not mean that the figurative cannot be used or implied; neither does it preclude the spiritual meaning. The literal meaning does not preclude application. Application is not the same as interpretation. John Calvin said, 'The Word of God is inexhaustible and applicable at all times, but there is a difference between explanation and application, application must be consistent with explanation.' 'There is one interpretation, but many applications.' This will be illustrated more as we progress.

3. Do not seek to find hidden meanings to the words of scripture when the meaning is obvious, or add to scripture (Revelation 22:18–19). Hidden meaning is not the same as depth of meaning. 'Some truths of scripture may patent, outward and obvious, whilst others are latent and inward and hidden. "Some historical events may have spiritual significance (such as Joseph's dream in Genesis 37) and certain figures of speech such as types and symbols, and parables and allegories may all have hidden meaning, but their meaning must be based on the earthly sense of the words and their interpretation must be within the boundaries of scripture."' For instance, Revelation 12—about the great sign of the woman clothed with the sun, with the moon under her feet and on her head a garland of twelve stars—is easily interpreted in the light of Joseph's dream in Genesis 37:9–10.

    'If the literal sense makes common sense, seek no other sense or we shall\ end up with non-sense.'

    Irvin L. Jensen, in his *A Self-Study Guide* (page 16), says of the *law of plain sense*: 'When the plain sense of scripture makes common sense, seek no other sense; therefore, take every word at its primary, ordinary, usual, literary meaning unless he facts of the context indicate otherwise.'

4. That prophecy can be understood just as it is without any changes or additions and that it is simply a record of things yet to happen sometime after its utterance.

5. It is not true that prophecy must be fulfilled before it can be understood. We have attempted to unravel many of the mysteries in the book of Revelation regarding the rapture of the church, the coming Antichrist and his empire, the battle of Armageddon, and many more future events, even though these are yet to happen. That is the essence of the message—to get you ready and prepared for what is prophesied to come

to pass. This is a season for preparing God's children for the Lord's coming, but many churches are preaching leadership, deliverance, and prosperity. If your members are harbouring sexual sins, bitterness, unforgiveness, and other lifestyles expressly forbidden by the scriptures, there is real danger that the Lord will leave such behind, with all their wealth and success and knowledge.

6. Do not interpret God's own interpretation of any symbol or prophecy or change the clear meaning of anything. God always explains His own symbols, and we must stay with those. For instance, God reveals that the angel who reveals the revelation to John was actually a man, a prophet of God, a servant like John (Revelation 1:1, 19:10, 22:8–9, 16).

Revelation 22:16 states: 'I, Jesus, have sent My angel to testify to you these things in the churches. I am the Root and the Offspring of David, the Bright and Morning Star.'

Revelation 22:8–9 states: 'Now I, John, saw and heard these things. And when I heard and saw, I fell down to worship before the feet of the angel who showed me these things. Then he said to me, "See *that you do* not *do that*. For I am your fellow servant, and of your brethren the prophets, and of those who keep the words of this book. Worship God."'

7. Bear this in mind when studying the book of Revelation: many signs and symbols are used in the book, but they are all explained either immediately where they are used, elsewhere in the same book, or somewhere in the Bible. For example, the Bible talks about seven stars and seven lampstands in Revelation 2, 3 and explains what the stars and the lampstands are in Revelation 1:20: 'The mystery of the seven stars which you saw in My right hand, and the seven golden lampstands: The seven stars are the angels of the seven churches, and the seven lampstands which you saw are the seven churches.'

Hebrews 2:16 states: 'For indeed He does not give aid to angels, but He does give aid to the seed of Abraham.'

Psalm 91:12 states: 'In *their* hands they shall bear you up, Lest you dash your foot against a stone.'

Here we see that Jesus' ministry is to humans and people, not to angels. Angels are His servants, so He will not carry an angel in His hands, but he does humans. This leads us to conclude that the angels to which the seven letters are addressed in the letters to the seven churches are the pastors or leaders of those churches. As a pastor, it is sobering to know that the Lord carries me in His right hand.

Also note that in addition to using *angel* to refer to ministers of the gospel over local churches and also to believers, it is also used to refer to angelic beings who serve God and the Lamb (Revelation 5:11, 7:11–12) and to the Lord Jesus Christ as the Jehovah Angel.

In Daniel 2:32–33, Daniel reveals King Nebuchadnezzar's dream and interprets it. The visions and dreams in the book covering the Gentile powers from Daniel's day to the Second Coming of Christ are all explained clearly in the book itself. Thus, the head of gold on the image (Daniel 2:32, 35, 38) and the lion (Daniel 7:4, 12, 17) symbolise Babylon, Nebuchadnezzar's kingdom (Daniel 2:37, 38; Jeremiah 15:4, 24:9, 25:11–12, 29:18). The breast and arms of silver on the image and the bear symbolise Medo-Persia, which followed Babylon in the times of the Gentiles. The belly and thighs of brass on the image and the leopard symbolise the old Grecian Empire of Alexander the Great, which followed Medo-Persia in the times of the Gentiles. The legs of iron and the indescribable beast symbolise the old Roman Empire that followed Greece and its four divisions. The feet and toes of iron and clay on the image and the ten horns on the indescribable beast represent the ten kings who will head ten kingdoms inside the old Roman Empire in the days of the Second Coming of Christ. Similarly, Revelation 17:1 says, 'Come and I will show you the judgement of the great harlot who sits on many waters.' And verse 15 continues: 'The waters which you saw, where the harlot sits, are peoples, multitudes, nations, and tongues.' In the same way, the woman sitting on a scarlet beast (Revelation 17:3) is explained in verse 18 as the great city which reigns over the kings of the earth—Babylon the Great, the capital city and the religious headquarters of the Antichrist. These are but a few examples of the Bible interpreting its own symbols in the immediate context.

8. Give only one meaning to a passage, the plain meaning, unless it is clear that another meaning is intended. There are instances where a double application is intended, but this would be clear from the context.

9. The two laws to understand in prophecy are:

    A) *The law of double reference.* In some passages, two distinct persons are referred to:

    • the visible person addressed
    • the invisible person who is using the visible person as a tool.

    For example, in Genesis 3:14–15, the serpent, the tool of the invisible Satan, is addressed, but it also refers to Satan, who is to meet defeat by the seed of the woman. In both Isaiah 14:4–27 and Ezekiel 28:112–19, the kings of Babylon and Tyre are addressed respectively, but Satan is also addressed as falling 'from heaven' for invading heaven to be like the Most High (Isaiah 14:12–14). You can tell that these statements could not possibly be referring to the visible person and referring to the invisible person in the same breath, because the human king of Tyre has never been to heaven nor does he have any way to invade it.

B) *The law of prophetic perspective. This refers to the description of future events as if they are continuous and successive events but may actually be thousands of years apart. For example, Isaiah 61:1–3 is recorded in Luke 4:17–20, where Christ stopped the prophecy at the words 'the acceptable year of the Lord', and then closed the book and said, 'This day is this scripture fulfilled in your ears.' But look at the whole prophecy, which goes on to say, 'And the day of vengeance of our God', which is actually 2,000 years to come, as that belongs to the tribulation of the end. At the Second Coming of Christ, He will come as the conquering warrior king with His heavenly armies and with vengeance to punish His enemies for their sins and rebellion, but this was not His mission during His first coming. At His first coming, He came to preach the good news to the poor, to heal the sick, to proclaim liberty to the captives, to restore sight to the blind (both literally and spiritually), to set the oppressed free, and to proclaim the acceptable year of the Lord, the time of God's abundant grace and favour for all mankind. It would have been untrue for Him to have read that part and claim that it is fulfilled in their ears. Even though both events are reported in the same sentence, one part has been fulfilled long ago while the other awaits its certain fulfilment.*

Another example of prophetic perspective is found in *John 5:25, 28–29*, where it says the dead will hear His voice and come forth. But we know that all the dead will not resurrect at the same time. There is at least a thousand years separating the resurrection of the righteous dead (the first resurrection) and that of the wicked dead (the second death). The righteous dead will resurrect during the rapture and the tribulation saints closer to the end of the tribulation to complete the first resurrection, but the wicked dead do not rise until the end of the millennium when they are called to appear at the great white throne judgement for sentencing prior to being sent into the lake of fire, which is the second death. These two events are separated by at least a thousand years. The first resurrection happens at the beginning of the one thousand years, while the second resurrection happens at the end. The first resurrection will involve only God's saints, while the second will involve both the wicked, unbelieving humans as well as all rebellious angels and spirits. The period between the first and the second resurrections is what is known as the millennium (Daniel 12:2; Acts 24:15; Corinthians 15:23–25, 28).

Revelation 20:4–6 says in verse 5: 'But the rest of the dead did not live again until the thousand years were finished. This is the first resurrection.'

The wicked dead appear later (in verse 12): 'And I saw the dead, small and great standing before God.' This is at the great white throne judgement (Daniel 12:2).

10. It is important to understand the history of the writer and the times and the circumstances in which the prophet lived and wrote and the people to whom he wrote (and how they understood his message) and the purpose of his message. For instance, in Revelation 12:1, the Bible records a great sign appearing in heaven: a woman clothed with the sun, with the moon under her feet, and on her head, a garland of twelve stars. First the Bible says this is a sign, meaning it is a symbol of something rather than a literal woman and literal sun and literal moon and stars. They each stand for something else. But there is no need to speculate for the meaning outside the Bible. Remember Joseph's second dream (Genesis 37:9), in which the sun, the moon, and the eleven stars bowed down to him. When his father, Jacob, heard of the dream, he rebuked him, saying, 'What is this dream that you have dreamed? Shall your mother and I and your brothers indeed come to bow down to the earth before you?' The patriarch Jacob clearly

understood his son Joseph's dream. Remember that Jacob was the father of the twelve tribes and hence of the Jewish nation. This clearly indicates that the woman spoken of in Revelation 12 is the nation of Israel, who gives birth to the 144,000 Jewish evangelists whom God will use in evangelising the world after the rapture of the church (Revelation 7, 14). This is a future event, as are all events from Revelation 4 onwards.

11. See the prophet primarily as a preacher of righteousness, a forth teller and a foreteller with powers of insight and foresight. The prophets Isaiah, Jeremiah, and Ezekiel and the minor prophets were mostly preachers of righteousness and foretelling, even though there were many prophecies of future events in their books, but Daniel and John were primarily foretelling future events and also with some aspects of foretelling messages.

In this sense, it is important not to see prophecy any different from the rest of scripture and assume that you need special education to understand it. It is nonetheless true that people may have special insight to certain aspects of scriptures by virtue of their calling and the ministry office in which they stand. This does not preclude any member of the body of Christ from studying and understanding the scriptures because at the end of the day, every believer has the indwelling Holy Spirit, the divine author of the Word of God.

Having said that, the body of Christ must learn to outsource specialist ministries and giftings so that their particular group may not be deprived of a vital truth. There is need for greater networking across ministries and churches. We must come to the understanding that we are one body working for the same master and that the people in your church and ministry are really not yours but the Lord's. With that understanding and openness, what is the point of poaching one another's sheep? And sheep that would easily follow another shepherd are really rebellious sheep—goats in sheep's clothing.

THE TIMES OF
THE GENTILES

The Old Testament word *gentiles* (Hebrew: *goy*) means 'a foreign nation', a 'non-Israelite'. The word *grecian* or *greek* has also been used to refer to a non-Jew, as also has *heathen*.

THE SOURCE OF THE DIFFERENT NATIONS

Before the flood of Noah, there were different families on earth, but after the flood, all the people of the earth descended from the three sons of Noah: Shem, Ham, and Japheth (according to Genesis 10; 1 Chronicles 1:5–7). Before Abraham, the human race was one, with one language, but all this changed at Babel, when God confused their tongues and scattered them abroad into separate nations with their own distinct territories and languages. Up till this time, God dealt with the human race as one people. But from Genesis 12, God chose Abraham to raise a race of people, a nation, whom He would deal directly with and who would in turn be used to evangelise all other nations.

This gave rise to two classes of people in scripture: the Hebrews or Israelites or Jews and the non-Israelites or the Gentiles. Now, God was going to give His Word to the Jews and teach them His ways. They were in turn to teach these to the Gentiles, with whom God was not going to deal directly henceforth. From observing these people, the Jews, the rest of mankind would learn the blessings from God for obeying Him and the curses and punishments that follow disobedience. And it is incredible how Israel has modelled this to the rest of mankind, in both the positive and negative sense.

When the New Testament church was born with the coming of the Holy Spirit on the day of the Pentecost (Acts 2), a third class of people was born, the church of Jesus Christ. Henceforth, we have the Jews, the Gentiles, and the church. The church was composed of Jews and Gentiles who have made Jesus Christ their Lord and Saviour.

> Therefore, whether you eat or drink, or whatever you do, do all to the glory of God. Give no offense, either to the Jews or to the Greeks or to the church of God, just as I also please all *men* in all *things,* not seeking my own profit, but the *profit* of many, that they may be saved.
> (1 Corinthians 10:31–32)

God not only sees these people groups as distinct, but he deals with them differently, and they have different destinies waiting for each of them. All the people descended through the patriarch Abraham; Isaac and Jacob are classified as Jews. All those who are not Jews and have also not accepted Jesus Christ as Lord and Saviour of their souls are classified as Gentiles. Anyone, whether Jew or Gentile, who accepts Jesus as their Lord and Saviour becomes a part of the church. Israel is awaiting a promised natural kingdom on earth in fulfilment of God's promises to their fathers. This will happen at the end of the seven-year tribulation after they have been taken through a time of severe trial and testing in the tribulation. The church of God will be raptured to be with God in heaven just prior to the tribulation but would eventually return to earth to rule and reign with Christ on earth for a thousand years and then for all eternity. All Gentiles who do not accept Christ as their Lord and Saviour during their lifetime on earth would eventually be consigned to hell and then, after the final judgement, to the lake of fire, which the Bible calls the second death.

THE MEANING OF THE TIMES OF THE GENTILES (LUKE 21:24; ROMANS 11:25; REVELATION 11:2)

And they will fall by the edge of the sword, and be led away captive into all nations. And Jerusalem will be trampled by Gentiles until the times of the Gentiles are fulfilled.

(Luke 21:24)

For I do not desire, brethren, that you should be ignorant of this mystery, lest you should be wise in your own opinion, that blindness in part has happened to Israel until the fullness of the Gentiles has come in.

(Romans 11:25)

But leave out the court which is outside the temple, and do not measure it, for it has been given to the Gentiles. And they will tread the holy city underfoot for forty-two months.

(Revelation 11:2)

This refers to that period of time from the beginning of Israel's history (in Egypt) to the Second Coming of Christ, during which time Israel has been more or less oppressed by Gentile nations. It is to do with the oppression of Israel, whether in or out of the land by Gentile nations. It is the same as the fullness of the Gentiles in Romans 11:25. It is not to do with the salvation of the Gentiles, because Gentile salvation continues through the tribulation and even in the millennium (Acts 2:16–21; Romans 10; Revelation 6:9–11, 7:9–17, 15:2–4, 20:4–6; Isaiah 2:4–65, 2:7, 66:19–24). It is the period of time from Israel's first to her last oppression by Gentile nations, whether they are in the land or not. You can see this oppression of Israel ratcheted up even today all around you, especially in the United Nations and in most nations of the world. It started with Israel's first oppression, being bondage in Egypt, where they first became a nation (Exodus 1) and will continue till her last at the eighth Grecian kingdom of the Antichrist when Christ comes to set up His millennial kingdom. In Revelation 11:1, 2, it is stated that Jerusalem will be trodden down during the last forty-two months or three and a half years of this age, during which time the Antichrist would be ruling and reigning over the nations of the Old Roman Empire directly from—guess where—Jerusalem (Daniel 8:13–14). Notice how the whole world is fighting over the status of Jerusalem today. It takes spiritual insight to know that this is not a mere controversy but a raging and intense spiritual battle, because Jerusalem is where Jesus would rule the nations from when He comes to establish His earthly kingdom. And Satan will contest this to the last man standing. It will end at the conclusion of Daniel's seventieth week, when Jesus returns to liberate the nation and His city and restore it to His personal and direct rule.

This means that the times of the Gentiles run through the Egyptian, Assyrian, Babylonian, Medo-Persian, Grecian, and the Roman empires. It will continue through the two empires yet, the future revised Roman Empire and the revived Grecian Empire, which will be the one ruled by the Antichrist and the one which will fight Christ at Armageddon at His Second Coming.

It is important to remember that since each succeeding empire took over the territory of the preceding one, the last empire, the revived Grecian Empire, will essentially include most of the elements and territories and peoples of all the preceding empires. This is very important because it helps us understand which nations will become part of the Antichrist's kingdom in the tribulation.

For instance, in Revelation 13:1–3, talking about the coming revival of the old Grecian Empire, the apostle saw it as a beast having seven heads (the seven empires that have preceded it) and ten horns (the ten constituent nations or kingdoms that will comprise the core of the beast kingdom).

> Then I stood on the sand of the sea. And I saw a beast rising up out of the sea, having seven heads and ten horns, and on his horns ten crowns, and on his heads a blasphemous name. Now the beast which I saw was

like a leopard, his feet were like *the feet of* a bear, and his mouth like the mouth of a lion. The dragon gave him his power, his throne, and great authority. And I saw one of his heads as if it had been mortally wounded, and his deadly wound was healed. And all the world marveled and followed the beast.

The beast itself was a leopard, which, according to Daniel's visions, symbolised the Grecian Empire, but it had the feet of a bear, which symbolised the Medo-Persian Empire, and had a mouth like a lion, which symbolised the Babylonian Empire. So you see how all these ancient empires would be embodied in the final Grecian Empire to do what they do best at the end of the age—to oppress Israel and the Jewish nation.

Here is the mind which has wisdom: The seven heads are seven mountains on which the woman sits. There are also seven kings. Five have fallen, one is, and the other has not yet come. And when he comes, he must continue a short time. The beast that was, and is not, is himself also the eighth, and is of the seven, and is going to perdition.

(Revelation 17:9–11)

The seven heads on the beast represent the seven the kingdoms which were coexistent with Israel from the beginning of her history till the beast, who is the eighth and last kingdom. So the beast is the eighth and final kingdom to oppress Israel, and he will have seven heads, which represent all the seven kingdoms or empires which preceded the eighth. This simply means all the seven preceding kingdoms will be in the eighth as to territory and peoples, as explained above.

EGYPT

Egypt was the first kingdom to oppress Israel in the times of the Gentiles and is represented by the first mountain. This simply means that Egypt will be in the kingdom of the Antichrist, according to Daniel 11:42–43. Egypt will be one of the four divisions of Greece and one of the ten of Rome in the last days (Daniel 7:24, 8:21–25). The Antichrist is called pharaoh, or king, of Egypt in Ezekiel 32:31 because he will rule over Egypt. It was in Egypt that Israel first became a nation, and they were enslaved by their cruel pharaohs till God Himself intervened with a spectacular deliverance.

ASSYRIA

Assyria was the second world power to oppress Israel in the times of the Gentiles. The Assyrian Empire, founded by Nimrod, comprised northern Iraq and southern Turkey.

> Cush begot Nimrod; he began to be a mighty one on the earth. He was a mighty hunter before the Lord; therefore it is said, 'Like Nimrod the mighty hunter before the Lord.' And the beginning of his kingdom was Babel, Erech, Accad, and Calneh, in the land of Shinar. From that land he went to Assyria and built Nineveh, Rehoboth Ir, Calah, and Resen between Nineveh and Calah (that is the principal city).
>
> (Genesis 10:8–12)

The Antichrist is called the Assyrian in Hosea:

> He shall not return to the land of Egypt; But the Assyrian shall be his king, Because they refused to repent.
>
> (Hosea 11:5)

When the Assyrian comes into our land, And when he treads in our palaces, Then we will raise against him Seven shepherds and eight princely men. They shall waste with the sword the land of Assyria, And the land of Nimrod at its entrances; Thus He shall deliver us from the Assyrian, When he comes into our land And when he treads within our borders. (Micah 5:5–6)

Because he will rule the land of Assyria, which will be part of the beast's empire as to territory and peoples. Assyria's downfall is prophesied because of her oppression of Israel in the last days (Isaiah 10:20–27, 14:25, 31:4–9; Micah 5:5–6).

BABYLON

Babylon (Iraq) was the third world kingdom to oppress Israel. It is the first mentioned in the book of Daniel 2, 7 and is symbolised by the head of gold and the lion with eagle's wings. Babylon will be in the Antichrist's kingdom at the coming of Christ.

MEDO-PERSIA

Medo-Persia (Iran) was the fourth kingdom to oppress and persecute Israel and the second recorded in Daniel. Medo-Persia is symbolised by the breast and arms of silver in Daniel 2, as the bear in Daniel 7, and as the ram in Daniel 8. It is worth noting that until 1936, ancient Persia comprised what is today known as Iran, Afghanistan, and Pakistan. It is not far-fetched to speculate that all three will be in the Antichrist's kingdom, judging by their common Islamic ties and their ominous posture towards the Jewish nation. Also note that Cyrus, the Persian, is mentioned in prophecy as liberating the Jews from Babylonian captivity and decreeing the rebuilding of the temple and the city in Isaiah 44:28–45, to be fulfilled over two hundred years later in 2 Chronicles 36:19–23; Ezra 1:1–8. The fact that the beast 'has the mouth of a lion' and 'the feet of a bear', which in Daniel symbolises Babylon and Medo-Persia, shows that both would be ruled by the Antichrist in the last days. Today (March 2018), Iran, which is ancient Persia, is poised on the doorstep of Israel, following her involvement in the ongoing Syrian war. The Medes (known today as Kurds, of which there are about 20 million in total) are scattered between Turkey, Iraq, Iran, and Syria and are fighting for independence of their homeland.

GREECE

Greece was the fifth Gentile kingdom to oppress Israel and the third mentioned in Daniel, symbolised by the image as a 'kingdom of brass which shall bear rule over the whole earth' (Daniel 2:39) and 'a leopard with 4 heads, showing the 4 divisions of the kingdom, two of which oppressed Israel' (Daniel 7:6) and 'the he goat' with a notable horn between his eyes, symbolising Alexander the Great, the founder of the Greek Empire, (Daniel 8:5–9, 20–25, 11:1–3). When Alexander died, his kingdom was broken up into four divisions, headed by his four best generals, two of whom (Syria and Egypt) oppressed Israel. In Daniel 11, 12, there were wars between Egypt (the king of the south) and Syria (the king of the north) for over one hundred fifty years, beginning with the reign of Ptolemy I, king of Egypt, and Seleucus I, king of Syria, ending with Antiochus Epiphanes, the Syrian king who foreshadowed the Antichrist (Daniel 11:21–34).

This prophecy was to show from which one of the four divisions of Greece the Antichrist will come. In the last days, there will be wars between the king of the north (Syria) and the king of the south (Egypt), in Daniel 11:40–45, to show that the king of the north will be victorious, proving that the Antichrist will come from Syria (Daniel 11:35, 12:13). In Daniel 8:8, 9, 17–26, we have the four Grecian divisions that will exist in the last days as Greece, Turkey, Egypt, and Syria (2 Thessalonians 2:8, 9; Revelation 13:2; Daniel 7:11; Revelation 19:11–21; Isaiah 11:4; 2 Thessalonians 1:1–10, 2:8–9).

The fifth mountain kingdom is 'the head that was wounded to death, and his deadly wound was healed'. This would be the eighth kingdom, the Grecian Kingdom, which the Antichrist will rule over and which will fight Christ at Armageddon.

ROME

Rome was the sixth world empire to oppress Israel and the fourth mentioned in Daniel. Rome came to power over Palestine about 63 BC. This was symbolised on the beast 'that was' at the time of John, the apostle, who wrote the book of Revelation. In Daniel 2:31–45, it is the fourth kingdom, strong as iron, that succeeded Egypt, Assyria, Babylon, Medo-Persia, and Greece as the oppressor of Israel; it is seen in Daniel 7:7–27 as the fourth beast, dreadful and terrible and exceedingly strong and had ten horns. And behold, there came up among them another little horn.

> After this I saw in the night visions, and behold, a fourth beast, dreadful and terrible, exceedingly strong. It had huge iron teeth; it was devouring, breaking in pieces, and trampling the residue with its feet. It was different from all the beasts that were before it, and it had ten horns. 8 I was considering the horns, and there was another horn, a little one, coming up among them, before whom three of the first horns were plucked out by the roots. And there, in this horn, were eyes like the eyes of a man, and a mouth speaking pompous words.
> (Daniel 7:7–8)

In Daniel 9:26–27, Rome is alluded to as the destroyer of Jerusalem and the temple, referred to by Jesus in Matthew 24:1–3 and Luke 21:20–24 and partially fulfilled in AD 70.

But when you see Jerusalem surrounded by armies, then know that its desolation is near. Then let those who are in Judea flee to the mountains, let those who are in the midst of her depart, and let not those who are in the country enter her. For these are the days of vengeance, that all things which are written may be fulfilled. But woe to those who are pregnant and to those who are nursing babies in those days! For there will be great distress in the land and wrath upon this people. And they will fall by the edge of the sword, and be led away captive into all nations. And Jerusalem will be trampled by Gentiles until the times of the Gentiles are fulfilled.

(Luke 21:20–24)

THE REVISED ROMAN EMPIRE

This is the only one of the seven kingdoms that is in the future and will become a relentless persecutor of Israel under the leadership of the great whore or harlot (the false religion), which would rule the ten kingdoms of revised Rome until the middle of the week. Mystery Babylon, the great whore, will seek to suppress every religion that is not her own and will murder the saints of Jesus until she is drunk with their blood during the first three and a half years of the week. The scriptures revealing the persecution of Christians and Israel by the great whore and the ten kings before the Antichrist gets full power over them include Matthew 24:4–13; Mark 13:4–13; Revelation 6:9–11, 17:3–6. The Antichrist will continue the persecution of Christians and break his seven-year covenant with Israel and determine to exterminate them from the face of the earth (Daniel 7:21–22, 8:24–25, 9:27, 12:1–7; Matthew 24:15–31; Revelation 7:9–17).

But when you see Jerusalem surrounded by armies, then know that its desolation is near. Then let those who are in Judea flee to the mountains, let those who are in the midst of her depart, and let not those who are in the country enter her. For these are the days of vengeance, that all things which are written may be fulfilled. But woe to those who are pregnant and to those who are nursing babies in those days! For there will be great distress in the land and wrath upon this people. And they will fall by the edge of the sword, and be led away captive into all nations. And Jerusalem will be trampled by Gentiles until the times of the Gentiles are fulfilled.

Then one of the seven angels who had the seven bowls came and talked with me, saying to me, 'Come, I will show you the judgment of the great harlot who sits on many waters, with whom the kings of the earth committed fornication, and the inhabitants of the earth were made drunk with the wine of her fornication.'

So he carried me away in the Spirit into the wilderness. And I saw a woman sitting on a scarlet beast which was full of names of blasphemy, having seven heads and ten horns. The woman was arrayed in purple and scarlet, and adorned with gold and precious stones and pearls, having in her hand a golden cup full of abominations and the filthiness of her fornication. And on her forehead a name was written:

MYSTERY, BABYLON THE GREAT,
THE MOTHER OF HARLOTS
AND OF THE ABOMINATIONS
OF THE EARTH.

I saw the woman, drunk with the blood of the saints and with the blood of the martyrs of Jesus. And when I saw her, I marveled with great amazement.

(Revelation 17:1–6)

Egypt, Assyria, Babylon, Medo-Persia, Greece, old Rome, revised Rome, revived Greece.

THE TEN HORNS AND THE BEAST ITSELF

Daniel 7:23–24; Revelation 17:12–17; Daniel 2:40–45; 7:7–27; 8:8, 17–25; 9:26–27; 11:1–45; 12:1–13; 13:1–3; 17:8–11.

The Roman Empire is to exist as ten kingdoms in the last days before the revelation of both the Antichrist and Christ and will be overthrown by both, first by the Antichrist and then by Christ, at the battle of Armageddon. In Daniel 2:40–45, we see the first picture of

Rome as having two legs of iron and ten toes of iron and clay. Rome has never existed before as separate kingdoms, as symbolised by the ten toes, and must exist as such to fulfil the prophecy. Rome has existed before as two divisions, symbolised by the two legs of iron, representing the western and the eastern divisions of the empire. This will happen just prior to Christ's coming to earth to establish His kingdom to rule and reign forever. (Isaiah 9:6–7; Revelation 11:15). These ten toes on the two feet on the two legs represent ten kingdoms—five from the eastern and five from the western divisions of Rome—in some kind of loose federation (Daniel 7:7–27).

And then 'another little horn' called the beast (Daniel 7:11) will rise 'after them' and overthrow three of them (Greece, Turkey, and Egypt). This little horn will continue 'until the Ancient of days comes'. The ten kings will give their kingdoms and power to the eleventh, or the beast, and they together will destroy the great whore in the middle of the week. Three and a half years later, they will fight Christ at Armageddon (Revelation 17:12–17).

> And the ten horns which you saw on the beast, these will hate the harlot, make her desolate and naked, eat her flesh and burn her with fire. For God has put it into their hearts to fulfill His purpose, to be of one mind, and to give their kingdom to the beast, until the words of God are fulfilled.
>
> (Revelation 17:16–17)

One thing is clear: Greece, Turkey, Egypt, and Syria must be four of the ten kingdoms in order to fulfil Daniel 8 and 11, for the Antichrist comes out of one of these four original Grecian divisions to revive the old Grecian Empire. The beast, as the eighth kingdom, will be ruled by the personal, visible, and mortal human being, the Antichrist, and the impersonal, invisible, and immortal angel, the prince of Grecia.

> Repent therefore and be converted, that your sins may be blotted out, so that times of refreshing may come

28

from the presence of the Lord, and that He may send Jesus Christ, who was preached to you before, whom heaven must receive until the times of restoration of all things, which God has spoken by the mouth of all His holy prophets since the world began.

(Acts 3:19–21)

This scripture seems to be saying that before Jesus returns to the earth in His second advent, there will be a restoration or fulfilment of the prophetic word. One such word would be the restoration of Israel as a sovereign nation, gathered back in their ancestral homeland in unbelief. That process is still ongoing. Israel became a nation once again in 7 May 1948, raised as a banner for the nations, constantly in the news.

He will set up a banner for the nations, And will assemble the outcasts of Israel, And gather together the dispersed of Judah. From the four corners of the earth.

(Isaiah 11:12)

Not only that, but all the ancient nations that God had used to chastise Israel in the times of the Gentiles would also feature prominently in the end times. Today we hear all those ancient Middle Eastern nations making all the headlines, unfortunately, often for all the wrong reasons. These will be the very nations—joined by others, of course—who will constitute the beast's kingdom that will persecute Israel in the end and constitute the nucleus of nations that will go against Christ to fight Him at the battle of Armageddon. We see all these nations—Islamic, of course—set up exactly for that purpose, oppressing Israel and seeking ways for her total destruction. Now it is apparent the heavens have no more reason to withhold and keep Jesus much longer. Most of the players for his coming are in place, ready to rumble, as it were.

Due to the recent wars and instabilities in these ancient nations, multitudes of their nationals have poured into the West as refugees and taken shelter in most Western nations. All these new immigrants will have a crucial role to play in their host nations when the Islamic Antichrist makes his appearance on the world stage and begins his mission of world conquest. In particular, when he makes his mark mandatory, overzealous Muslim youths will go out of their way to try to enforce these, even in nations that are not directly under the rule of the Antichrist. The scene is set for the final drama of the ages, and it is important that everyone knows what side of the turf they stand, because you cannot play neutral in what is coming. Even if you don't make a choice, you will be forced to make a choice, one way or the other.

It is as if God is saying to all mankind today:

> I call heaven and earth as witnesses today against you, that I have set before you life and death, blessing and cursing; therefore choose life, that both you and your descendants may live; Seek the Lord while He may be found.
>
> (Deuteronomy 30:19)

> Call upon Him while He is near. Let the wicked forsake his way, And the unrighteous man his thoughts; Let him return to the Lord, And He will have mercy on him; And to our God, For He will abundantly pardon.
>
> (Isaiah 55:6–7)

THERE ARE WARS ON THE HORIZON: THE PSALM 83 AND EZEKIEL 38–39 WARS

End time experts are talking a lot about the Gog–Magog war of Ezekiel 38–39, a prophecy that predicts a powerful confederacy, apparently led by Russia, that is destined to someday invade Israel. Some think that its fulfilment is even knocking at our door, especially more so with Russia camped at the very doorstep of Israel, following their involvement in the war in Syria.

But a lesser-known prophecy is gaining momentum and importance for our day: Psalm 83, in which a different confederacy attempts to wipe out Israel.

This psalm seems to be addressing current issues in the Middle East—nations conspiring to destroy Israel. President Trump's recognition of Jerusalem as the capital of Israel on 6 December 2017 and efforts to move the US embassy from Tel Aviv to Jerusalem before the end of May 2019 could well be the event that triggers this war. I hope I am wrong, but all these, including the ancient prophecy, reads like today's headline news. What a time to be alive.

ASAPH'S VISION OF A FUTURE WAR

> O God, do not remain silent; do not turn a deaf ear, do
> not stand aloof, O God. See how your enemies growl,
> how your foes rear their heads.
>
> (Psalm 83:1–2)

Psalm 83 is more than a prayer or a plea to God for vengeance on Israel's enemies; it reveals that a ten-member confederacy wants to destroy the chosen people and possess the Promised Land, early historical Israel.

But Asaph was not just a worshiper, according to 2 Chronicles 29:30; he was also a *chozeh* (seer or prophet). As a prophet, Asaph saw beyond this period of peace to a time when this confederacy would seek the utter destruction of Israel. That time now seems to be nearing. "'Come,' they say, 'let us destroy them as a nation, so that Israel's name is remembered no more.'" (Psalm 83:4). Even though Asaph's vision was received in a time of peace, it must have been cause for some concern since many named in the confederacy had previously demonstrated their hatred towards Israel and the Jewish nation.

Of course, even today, conspiring against the Jewish people is considered nothing new. From the Philistines to the Nazis, the Jewish people have been plotted against. Death to Israel is some countries' national anthem. It is the one common thing that unites certain peoples on the earth, as if their lives would not have any meaning apart from seeking the total destruction of Israel.

> See how your enemies growl, how your foes rear their
> heads. With cunning they conspire against your people;
> they plot against those you cherish.
>
> (Psalm 83:2–3)

THE COALITION'S MOTIVE: BREAK
THE ABRAHAMIC COVENANT

> With one mind they plot together; they form an alliance
> against you.
>
> (Psalm 83:5)

The ten-member coalition of Psalm 83 forms a covenant with each other against not only the nation of Israel but the God of Israel. If one could destroy Israel, then the God of Israel, who has underwritten their safety and protection, is found to be a liar who cannot deliver on His Word.

The coalition is not satisfied to only destroy Israel as a nation; they want to wipe out the memory of the name of Israel, in effect, breaking the Abrahamic covenant.

In the Abrahamic covenant, God pledged that a chosen people would come through Abraham (*Genesis 22:17–18*), through Isaac (*Genesis 26:2–4*) and through Jacob (*Genesis 28:14*) and that God would give them the Promised Land of Canaan *(Genesis 15:18; Joshua 1:4)*.

THE TEN-MEMBER COALITION

While Israel's many enemies have wanted to destroy the nation of Israel and the Jewish people, Asaph specifically identifies ten nations/ groups that unite to form a coalition for this very purpose:

> With one mind they plot together; they form an alliance
> against you—the tents of Edom and the Ishmaelites,
> of Moab and the Hagrites, Byblos Gebal, Ammon and
> Amalek, Philistia, with the people of Tyre. Even Assyria
> has joined them to reinforce Lot's descendants.
>
> (Psalm 83:5–8)

While these groups are no longer identifiable by their ancient names, Bill Salus, author of *Israelistine* and *Psalm 83: The Missing Prophecy Revealed*, ascertains the modern-day equivalents/descendants of these coalition members as the following:

- Tents of Edom: Palestinians and southern Jordanians
- Ishmaelites: Saudis (Ishmael is the father of the Arabs)
- Moab: Palestinians and central Jordanians
- Hagrites: Egyptians (Hagar is the matriarch of Egypt)
- Gebal (Byblos): Hezbollah and northern Lebanese
- Ammon: Palestinians and northern Jordanians
- Amalek: Arabs of the Sinai area
- Philistia: Hamas of the Gaza Strip
- Tyre: Hezbollah and southern Lebanese
- Assyria: Syrians and northern Iraqis.

These nations are the immediate neighbours of Israel, and they are all Muslim.

THE COALITION'S GOAL: DESTROY ISRAEL

While this ten-member coalition might not yet be overtly united in an action against Israel, these nations do exists today and are already united under the values of Islam.

Moreover, Islam is influenced by a sibling rivalry that dates back to Ishmael and Isaac and then Esau and Jacob (Genesis 21:9–10, 27:41; Obadiah; Ezekiel 35:5).

> So the child grew and was weaned. And Abraham made a great feast on the same day that Isaac was weaned.
>
> And Sarah saw the son of Hagar the Egyptian, whom she had borne to Abraham, scoffing. Therefore she said to Abraham, 'Cast out this bondwoman and her son; for the son of this bondwoman shall not be heir with

my son, *namely* with Isaac.' And the matter was very displeasing in Abraham's sight because of his son.

But God said to Abraham, 'Do not let it be displeasing in your sight because of the lad or because of your bondwoman. Whatever Sarah has said to you, listen to her voice; for in Isaac your seed shall be called. Yet I will also make a nation of the son of the bondwoman, because he *is* your seed.'

So Abraham rose early in the morning, and took bread and a skin of water; and putting *it* on her shoulder, he gave *it* and the boy to Hagar, and sent her away. Then she departed and wandered in the Wilderness of Beersheba.

(Genesis 21:8–14)

So Esau hated Jacob because of the blessing with which his father blessed him, and Esau said in his heart, 'The days of mourning for my father are at hand; then I will kill my brother Jacob.'

(Genesis 27:41)

This ancient resentment against the chosen ones is perhaps fuelling the attacks and conspiracies against the existence of a Jewish homeland.

Of course, these Psalm 83 countries are actively conspiring today to either take over the land of Israel and make it their own or to prevent Israel from being a Jewish state. In other words, they want to make Israel a country that cannot protect and shelter the Jewish people from those who hate them.

Palestinians—Tents of Edom (Esau); Moab and Ammon (Sons of Lot)

Although Israel is currently in peace negotiations with the Palestinian Authority (PA) for a two-state solution, on 11 January 2014, the PA president, Mahmoud Abbas, made his intentions about Israel's existence clear:

> 'We won't recognize and accept the Jewishness of Israel. We have many excuses and reasons that prevent us from doing so,' Abbas said.

> 'We will march to Jerusalem in the millions, as free people and heroes,' he asserted.
>
> *(JPost)*

Jordanians—Tents of Edom; Moab and Ammon

Although Jordan and Israel have enjoyed a peace treaty since 1994, on 2 February 2014, Jordan's foreign minister Nasser Judeh told his parliament that Israel should not be recognized as a Jewish state nor should Jordan take in the Palestinian refugees ('tents of Edom').

In response, on 8 February 2014, Jordan's parliament voted to not recognize Israel as a Jewish state.

Hezbollah and Lebanon—Gebal (Byblos) and Tyre

On 2 August 2013, while Hezbollah, the terrorist group based in Lebanon, has been helping Syrian president Assad wage war against the rebels, its leader, Hassan Nasrallah, came out of hiding to remind the people of Lebanon that 'Israel poses a danger on all people of this region . . . including Lebanon, and removing it is a Lebanese national interest' *(JPost)*.

In February 2014, Nasrallah reinforced this idea, deceptively telling the Lebanese people, 'Israel is still an enemy and a threat to Lebanon's people, water, oil, security, and sovereignty.'

Hamas—Philistines

Although Gaza is officially a part of the Palestinian Authority, ruled by President Abbas, the terrorist group Hamas (meaning 'violence' in Hebrew) rules Gaza and is ready to form a coalition with any Muslim group willing to resist Israel.

Its charter states: 'Hamas will only be of help to all associations and organizations which act against the Zionist enemy and those who revolve in its orbit.'

In January 2014, Hamas interior minister Fathi Hamad said that the goal of Hamas is the total destruction of Israel.

> 'We are coming after the Zionists with all our leaders and soldiers,' Hamad said. 'You have only eight years on the land of Palestine before your demise.'
>
> (*JPost*)

Egyptians (or Possibly Northern Jordanians)—Hagrites or Hagarenes

A year after the Muslim Brotherhood leadership in Egypt was overthrown in a coup, this country has been working to undermine the power of Gaza's Hamas.

With another coup or change of heart, Egypt is now well positioned for a southern attack on Israel.

Saudis (or All Arabs)—Ishmaelites

Today, Israel and Saudi Arabia are forging economic, military, and diplomatic ties, but only time will tell how long this will endure. It may well be because of Sunni Saudis' fear of Shia Iran and nothing else, and when that fear is removed, Saudi may well return to their age-old hatred for all that is Jewish. We wait to see the outcome of this new rapprochement between these two ancient enemies.

Prophecy expert and author Bill Salus believes Saudi Arabia represents the Ishmaelite people in Psalm 83. Like most Arabs throughout the Middle East and Africa, the Saudis claim to be the true chosen people (as descendants of Ishmael).

Nevertheless, Saudi Arabia voted no to the 1947 UN resolution to create a Jewish state, and they supported the Arab invasions of 1948, 1967, and 1973 with troops as well as finances. They do not have diplomatic relations with Israel.

Arabs of the Sinai (or of the Negev Area)— Amalek (Grandson of Esau)

Bill Salus places the Amalekites in Sinai. He believes they were a part of Esau's family (the Edomites) who migrated into the Sinai area, which is part of Egypt.

Others, however, think that the Amalekites originated near Mecca and, by the tenth century BC, migrated to the Negev area of modern Israel (WND). It is possible, therefore, that some Arab-Israelis currently enjoying citizenship within Israel are of this group.

Indeed, some Arabs inside Israel look for its destruction as a Jewish state and even have representation in the Knesset (parliament):

'Israel should be defined as a state of its own nationalities. There are two nationalities in Israel. One is [the] Jewish majority, one is [the] Arab-Palestinian minority,' said the deputy speaker of the Knesset Ahmad Tibi in

January 2014. 'Saying that Israel is the Jewish state is neglecting our existence, our very existence and our narrative, and I will not accept that,' he added.

(CBC)

Syrians and Northern Iraqis (and Possibly Turkey)—Assyria

Since the creation of both Israel and Syria in the mid twentieth century, diplomatic ties have never been established between these two countries, which share a border.

Syria has attacked Israel in three major wars—in 1948, 1967, and 1973. The situation in Syria is incredibly volatile today and is worsening by the day.

THE PROPHET APPEALS FOR VICTORY

In Psalm 83, the prophet Asaph appeals to God, asking Him to make the coalition members perish in disgrace (Psalm 83:9–18).

In fact, Obadiah (Ezekiel 25–27, 37:10) and Jeremiah (49:1–6) prophesy that these coalition members will indeed perish and be cursed. *Genesis 12:3* predicts: 'I will bless those who bless you, and whoever curses you I will curse; and all peoples on earth will be blessed through you.'

These connecting prophetic verses seem to refer to Israel's victory in Psalm 83.

God will use the IDF to defeat the invading confederacy and kill their leaders and take their women and their little ones captive. They will burn down some of their cities and take much booty (Numbers 31:1–11).

And they warred against the Midianites, just as the Lord commanded Moses, and they killed all the males. They killed the kings of Midian with the rest of those who were killed—Evi, Rekem, Zur, Hur, and Reba, the five kings of Midian. Balaam the son of Beor they also killed with the sword.

And the children of Israel took the women of Midian captive, with their little ones, and took as spoil all their cattle, all their flocks, and all their goods. They also burned with fire all the cities where they dwelt, and all their forts. And they took all the spoil and all the booty—of man and beast.

(Numbers 31:7–11)

It would be like Gideon subduing 120,000 Midianites with only 300 men.

When the three hundred blew the trumpets, the Lord set every man's sword against his companion throughout the whole camp; and the army fled to Beth Acacia, toward Zererah, as far as the border of Abel Meholah, by Tabbath.

And the men of Israel gathered together from Naphtali, Asher, and all Manasseh, and pursued the Midianites.

Then Gideon sent messengers throughout all the mountains of Ephraim, saying, 'Come down against the Midianites, and seize from them the watering places as far as Beth Barah and the Jordan.' Then all the men of Ephraim gathered together and seized the watering places as far as Beth Barah and the Jordan. And they captured two princes of the Midianites, Oreb and Zeeb. They killed Oreb at the rock of Oreb, and Zeeb they killed at the winepress of Zeeb. They pursued Midian and brought the heads of Oreb and Zeeb to Gideon on the other side of the Jordan.

(Judges 7:22–25)

They will be like Sisera, who fled before the pursuing army but was killed by a woman with a tent peg.

And the Lord routed Sisera and all his chariots and all his army with the edge of the sword before Barak; and Sisera alighted from his chariot and fled away on foot. But Barak pursued the chariots and the army as far as Harosheth Hagoyim, and all the army of Sisera fell by the edge of the sword; not a man was left.

However, Sisera had fled away on foot to the tent of Jael, the wife of Heber the Kenite; for there was peace between Jabin king of Hazor and the house of Heber the Kenite. And Jael went out to meet Sisera, and said to him, 'Turn aside, my lord, turn aside to me; do not fear.' And when he had turned aside with her into the tent, she covered him with a blanket.

Then he said to her, 'Please give me a little water to drink, for I am thirsty.' So she opened a jug of milk, gave him a drink, and covered him. And he said to her, 'Stand at the door of the tent, and if any man comes and inquires of you, and says, 'Is there any man here?' you shall say, 'No.''

Then Jael, Heber's wife, took a tent peg and took a hammer in her hand, and went softly to him and drove the peg into his temple, and it went down into the ground; for he was fast asleep and weary. So he died. And then, as Barak pursued Sisera, Jael came out to meet him, and said to him, 'Come, I will show you the man whom you seek.' And when he went into her tent, there lay Sisera, dead with the peg in his temple.

So on that day God subdued Jabin, king of Canaan in the presence of the children of Israel. And the hand of the children of Israel grew stronger and stronger against Jabin king of Canaan, until they had destroyed Jabin king of Canaan.

(Judges 4:15–24)

The war would be fought and won in the heavenlies, with the stars and heavenly bodies involved.

They fought from the heavens; The stars from their courses fought against Sisera. The torrent of Kishon swept them away, That ancient torrent, the torrent of Kishon. O my soul, march on in strength!

(Judges 5:20–21)

This is the essence of Asaphs's prayer. He appeals for God to be involved and to come to Israel as the forces mustered against her are far superior in numbers, and God will sure answer this prayer as He always has on Israel's behalf. Oreb and Zeeb were two princes of the Midianites who were captured and killed by Gideon's army. Like the whirling dust, the invaders will flee, and like chaff before the wind. The end result of this ill-fated invasion of Israel is that the invaders will be humiliated in defeat, ashamed and surprised at what has hit them, and come to know that the God of Abraham, Isaac, and Jacob is the one and only true God and that Allah is not God nor the equal of God. They will know that Jehovah is the true God, the Lord God Almighty. The end result is that Israel will get its temple back. Victory for Israel will mean massive worldwide revival for the church and the world.

Well, you say, 'But Israel does not know it's God.' Well, it proves God's grace and enduring faithfulness.

According to Genesis 15:18–21:

On the same day the Lord made a covenant with Abram, saying:

'To your descendants I have given this land, from the river of Egypt to the great river, the River Euphrates—the Kenites, the Kenezzites, the Kadmonites, the Hittites, the Perizzites, the Rephaim, the Amorites, the Canaanites, the Girgashites, and the Jebusites.'

And if God continues to be faithful to His covenant with the fathers of the Jewish people, you can be sure that He will continue to be faithful to His New covenant with you established on the precious blood of His Son, Jesus Christ.

THE FATE OF THE INVADERS

- Edom (Palestinians, descendants of Esau) Obadiah 1:17–18
- Ammon (Palestinians and northern Jordanians) Ezekiel 25:13–17
- Tyre (Hezbollah and southern Jordanians) Ezekiel 26:1–6; 19–21
- Egypt (Hagrites) Ezekiel 29:8–15
- Syria/Damascus Isaiah 17:1–14.

Damascus will cease to exist as a city after over five thousand years of continuous human habitation, possibly through an Israeli nuclear blast.

According to Ezekiel 35:10, God says that if any nation should know the truth of the gospel and God's redemption plan for all mankind and His Son, Jesus Christ, as Lord, it should be the descendants of Ishmael and the Arab nation because their fathers grew up in the tents of Abraham. They must have been told the truth of God's redemptive plan through Abraham, Isaac, Jacob, and the Jewish people. God loved Ishmael and blessed him abundantly with material blessings. The massive wealth these nations have enjoyed is not an accident of history but of God's blessing to them because of their descent from Abraham.

Also the text says they want to take over the tiny slither of land left for the Jewish people, although the Lord was there. They were eyewitnesses of Jesus' ministry and the history of Christianity, Paul having gone to Damascus and the surrounding nations. Even in Old Testament times, it was to these same places that God sent His servants—Abraham, Isaac, Jacob, Jonah, Daniel, Joseph, the early apostles, and many others—to reveal Himself to them. But they have chosen hatred over love, falsehood over truth. How sad. We hope that after this crushing and humiliating military defeat, many of them will think hard about the course they have been following and come to Jesus and be saved, because God wants to save the descendants of Ishmael.

In their humiliation, the invaders will come to realise that the God of Israel—the God of Abraham, Isaac, and Jacob—alone is the true God and the only one to be worshipped. They will realise finally that Allah is not God but a false pretender who cannot deliver on his promises. They will not understand what actually hit them. How come Allah has not delivered victory to them? It has taken a very long time to come to this realisation, but finally they will get the message, and many of them will put their trust in Israel's God for salvation. This war will so devastate the heartlands of Islam that it will hardly recover as a world-conquering religion. All talk of ruling the world, which is loud and clear in the politico-religious circles, will dim to a whimper, and it is only a matter of one more devastating military defeat at the hands of Almighty God Himself in the Ezekiel 38–39 war to knock Islam completely off its perch for good as a global-menacing force.

Psalm 83:16–18 says:

> Fill their faces with shame, That they may seek Your name, O Lord. Let them be confounded and dismayed forever; Yes, let them be put to shame and perish, That they may know that You, whose name alone is the Lord, Are the Most High over all the earth.

God will do all these and some for Israel, not because they are good or better than any other nation, but to honour His covenant with their fathers and hallow His own name as He declares in Ezekiel 36:22–23, 32.

Therefore say to the house of Israel 'Thus says the Lord God: 'I do not do this for your sake, O house of Israel, but for My holy name's sake, which you have profaned among the nations wherever you went. And I will sanctify My great name, which has been profaned among the nations, which you have profaned in their midst; and the nations shall know that I am the Lord,' says the Lord God, 'when I am hallowed in you before their eyes.

(Ezekiel 36:22–23)

After this war, Israel will occupy a much-extended territory and achieve regional military and economic superiority, becoming one of the wealthiest nations, if not the wealthiest, on the planet. But all this is setting her up for another devastating war shortly afterwards.

EZEKIEL 38–39 WAR: THE WAR OF GOG AND MAGOG

A resulting sense of regional security and unparalleled economic prosperity following its overwhelming victory in the Psalm 83 war may make Israel ripe for the battle of Ezekiel 38–39—the invasion of a multi-membered coalition whose leaders say,

> I will go up against the land of unwalled villages. I will fall upon the quiet people who dwell securely, all of them dwelling without walls, and having no bars or gates, to seize spoil and carry off plunder.
>
> (Ezekiel 38:11–12)

While Israel today is indeed prospering and is a safe country to visit, she will have incredible riches and wealth and live in unparalleled safety after the victory of Psalm 83 is complete.

Since none of Israel's recent wars with her Islamic neighbours precisely fulfil this prophecy, we can understand that some future war involving a large coalition of nations in the outer ring of Israel's neighbours will fulfil it.

Today that coalition, which is united under the common values and motives of Islam, fits the prophecy's requirements like no other time in history. In the last couple of years and months, military pacts and alliances are being formed between countries, which would have been nigh impossible only a decade ago.

Therefore, many believe the war in Psalm 83 will happen soon to set the stage for the invasion of Ezekiel 38–39. In fact, none of the ten coalition members of Psalm 83 are mentioned in Ezekiel 38–39, though the book of Ezekiel mentions them elsewhere. This is so possibly because those nations might well have been obliterated by the Psalm 83 war.

The nations listed in the Ezekiel 38–39 war:

These nations are called by their ancient names and can be traced to their ancestry and the historical geographical locations.

> Now the word of the Lord came to me, saying, 'Son of man, set your face against Gog, of the land of Magog, the prince of Rosh, Meshech, and Tubal, and prophesy against him, and say, 'Thus says the Lord God: Behold, I am against you, O Gog, the prince of Rosh, Meshech, and Tubal.
>
> (Ezekiel 38:1–3)

> Persia, Ethiopia and Libya[b] are with them, all of them with shield and helmet; Gomer and all its troops; the house of Togarmah from the far north and all its troops—many people are with you.
>
> (Ezekiel 38:5–6)

Meshech, Gomer, Tubal, and Togarmah are all provinces of modern-day Turkey.

Magog very likely is a reference to the Turkish-speaking nations of the former Soviet Union, which includes Kazakhstan, Turkmenistan, Kyrgyzstan, Tajikistan, and possibly Afghanistan. It is worth noting that all these are Islamic nations and sworn enemies of the state of Israel.

Persia, which is modern Iran, is a key player in this war. It is worth noting that until 1935, the Persian Empire consisted of Iran, Afghanistan, and Pakistan. These countries might all be involved in this war since all are radically Islamic and shared a vitriolic hatred for the Jewish state and would enthusiastically throw their lot behind any coalition they believe is going to destroy their sworn enemy once and for all.

Ethiopia is listed as one of the nations, but this is translated from Cush, which actually refer to the land south of Egypt, which we identify as Sudan, another radical Islamic republic which will happily join such an enterprise.

Put is listed as one of the nations and may actually refer to but is not limited to Libya but many of the North African Islamic nations, like Algeria, Morocco, Tunisia, Mauritania, etc.

They will all be led, guided, and equipped by Rosh, Russia, which is the leader of the invading force. It is worth noting that Russia, though a secular state, has a very large and growing Muslim population and her armed forces are heavily Islamic. Also, Russia has, in the last couple of years, forged close military alliances with most of these Islamic nations against the West. Notable among them are Iran and Turkey. Turkey was a long-standing ally of Israel, but following President Erdogan's accession to power, there has been a massive shift towards making her an Islamic state and towards aligning with Russia against the West, even though she still retains her NATO membership. Russia is the nation that will come from the extreme north. Never in history has Russia come into any alliance with Iran and Turkey, but it is happening right now. The events of history have conspired to bring all these nations ominously to the doorsteps of Israel as we speak. They have all come to fight ISIS in Syria and Iraq. But with ISIS defeated, these nations are now busy establishing a longer-term military presence in Syria, virtually guaranteeing this war in the near future. More importantly, Russia just announced, on March 2018, to protect all things Syrian. This means that any Israeli retaliation against a Syrian or Iranian atrocity against Israel will be considered as an aggression against Russia, to which the Israeli prime minister Benyamin Netanyahu has rightly and characteristically responded defiantly. See all these in the context of a weak and abdicating US foreign policy, which literally abandoned the Middle East under the Obama regime. Obama literally handed the Middle East to the Russians and the Iranians, in particular, but this is not the end of the story, because it is only the counsel of the Lord that will ultimately prevail. Let history be the judge.

Slowly but surely, Iran is taking over most of the Muslim world and currently controls Syria, Iraq, and Lebanon, where Hizbollah, their proxy army, is in charge as well as many of the Islamic terror groups, to the trepidation of Egypt and Saudi Arabia. The situation is so bad that Egypt and Saudi are currently forging all kinds of alliances with Israel just to protect them from the Iranian menace.

These are the conditions in Israel at the time of the invasion: Israel will be dwelling securely or safely. This may be the aftermath of Israel's comprehensive victory over its immediate Islamic neighbours in the Psalm 83 war, as declared in Ezekiel 38:8.

Israel will be a people dwelling without walls. They may have let down their guard militarily, following a sense of military invincibility. Recently, the Israeli prime minister announced in the UN, 'Israel has never been stronger' (Ezekiel 37:10). While that may be true, the leaders of Israel might as well recognise that it is the God of their fathers—the God of Abraham, Isaac, and Jacob—who has protected them against all odds thus far. Yes, they may be strong militarily, but they should not trust in their military might alone because however you look at it, the odds have always been heavily stacked against Israel. This overconfidence could be a false security, and never at any time should Israel let down their guard until the last war of Armageddon is over. Thence, they will dwell secure. Until then, desolations are still determined for her.

They will acquire great plunder in addition to taking over much of the land occupied by the Arabs today, according to Obadiah1:9 and Jeremiah 49:2.

They will be enjoying sovereign international acclaim (Ezekiel 25:14, 38:14,16) for their economic and technological feats, which have been nothing short of breathtaking.

They will be a nation at peace in the Middle East, as unbelievable as that may sound today. While Israel may still be a peaceful nation to live in, one cannot say that Israel is living at peace at the moment. This peace will happen just after the Psalm 83 war when she has taken over most of the region, with many of the leaders of these nations dead or deposed (Ezekiel 28:25, 26).

Israel will live in the midst of the land. This may be a reference to the fact that Israel will be sitting pretty in their much-expanded territory. After Psalm 83, the land of Israel will approximate that which God promised to their fathers. It may also be a reference to the fact that Israel will be a global centre of innovation and enterprise and literally be the centre of the world for most of the technology that drives industrial and technological innovation today. Israel is already a leader in much of the cutting-edge innovation and technology in the world today. With her recent discovery of one of the world's largest deposits of natural gas in the Leviathan offshore and Tamar gas fields near Haifa and large quantities of oil in the Golan Heights near their border with Syria, Israel is bound to be a very wealthy, if not the wealthiest, nation on the earth (Zephaniah 2:7–9). I believe God has saved His best for His covenant people, because it is unforeseeable that God will bless all the sons of Abraham who dwell in the Arabian peninsula and the Gulf States with so much wealth and leave the descendants of Isaac out. Like all things God, you inherit His promises only by faith and patience. No more shall it be said that of all the places in the land of Canaan, Moses settled on the one spot without oil.

From the above descriptions of the economic conditions in Israel, it is not surprising why Russia will be eyeing Israel with jealousy and hatred. She will simply want her hands on Israel's oil and gas wealth and industrial and innovative capital. But why does Russia need all these allies to attack Israel? It is because by this time, Israel has become a strong, powerful, and mighty army.

According to Ezekiel 37:9–10:

> Also He said to me, 'Prophesy to the breath, prophesy,
> son of man, and say to the breath, "Thus says the Lord
> God: 'Come from the four winds, O breath, and breathe
> on these slain, that they may live.'"' So I prophesied as
> He commanded me, and breath came into them, and

they lived, and stood upon their feet, an exceedingly great army.

This is an end time war, coming in the last days, or the time just before the return of the Lord. It will take place after the regathering of Israel from the nations back to their land (Ezekiel 38:12). Some prophecy experts believe this war will happen at the beginning of the last three and a half years of the seven-year tribulation. That could well be the case, in which case her sense of security is the result of the seven-year peace treaty with the Antichrist. That makes perfect sense, but I believe this war will happen on the heels of the Psalm 83 victory and may be the response of the outer ring Islamic nations to the destruction of Damascus following the Psalm 83 war.

Isaiah prophesied:

> The burden against Damascus.
> 'Behold, Damascus will cease from being a city,
> And it will be a ruinous heap.'
>
> (Isaiah 17:1)

> Then behold, at eventide, trouble!
> And before the morning, he is no more.
> This is the portion of those who plunder us,
> And the lot of those who rob us.
>
> (Isaiah 17:14)

This may well be the hook into Gog's jaws that God uses to draw her to battle.

Motives for the invasion:

> You will say, 'I will go up against a land of unwalled villages; I will go to a peaceful people, who dwell safely, all of them dwelling without walls, and having neither bars nor gates'—to take plunder and to take booty, to stretch out your hand against the waste places that are

again inhabited, and against a people gathered from the nations, who have acquired livestock and goods, who dwell in the midst of the land. Sheba, Dedan, the merchants of Tarshish, and all their young lions will say to you, 'Have you come to take plunder? Have you gathered your army to take booty, to carry away silver and gold, to take away livestock and goods, to take great plunder?'

(Ezekiel 38:11–13)

It is obvious that this attack is motivated by the evil hatred and jealousy these people have for Israel (Ezekiel 38:10, 14).

They come to plunder Israel's wealth and to take booty (Ezekiel 38:12, 13b).

They want to take over the land, including the settlements, and establish another Islamic republic.

They will cover the land like a cloud, Gog and many peoples with him. This will be a massive assembly of nations and peoples against the tiny Israel.

But really, God says it is He who lures Gog and his troops to the land of Israel to exact retribution on them. He says in Ezekiel 38: 'I will turn you around, and put hooks in your jaws, and lead you out, with your army, horses, and horsemen, all splendidly clothed, a great company with bucklers and shields, all of them handling swords.' He continues, 'After many days, you will be visited' (Ezekiel 38:8a). In verse 16, He continues, 'It will be in the latter days that I will bring you against My land.' God continues in 39:2: 'And I will turn you around and lead you on' really like a baited animal.'

So perhaps, instead of being so hard on the ex-president Obama and his administration for abandoning Israel and the Middle East to Iran and Russia, we should really see the hand and plan of God in all this. At the end of the day, God is the ultimate keeper of Israel, even though more often than not He does so through human instruments, which role America should be privileged to embrace and for her own good.

The world's response to the invasion: This will at best be muted condemnations and protest in the UN, but there will be no real effort to stop the invasion. Sheba, Dedan, the merchants of Tarshish, and all their young lions will condemn the invasion, possibly in the chambers of the UN. Tarshish may be a reference to the United Kingdom, and her young lions will be the young Commonwealth nations, which retains the queen of Britain as their head of state.

Ezekiel 38:13 puts it this way:

> Sheba, Dedan, the merchants of Tarshish, and all their young lions will say to you, 'Have you come to take plunder? Have you gathered your army to take booty, to carry away silver and gold, to take away livestock and goods, to take great plunder?'

Perhaps that is also part of God's broader plan so that He alone will have the honour of defending and protecting Israel. God says that His face will show his fury over their actions to take over His land.

He will strike the invaders with a massive earthquake in the land of Israel, an earthquake that will be felt throughout the whole world by all earth dwellers, including man and beasts. The earthquake will be so massive it will literally rearrange the topography of the Middle East.

According to Ezekiel 38:18–22:

> 'And it will come to pass at the same time, when Gog comes against the land of Israel,' says the Lord God, 'that My fury will show in My face. For in My jealousy and in the fire of My wrath I have spoken: "Surely in that day there shall be a great earthquake in the land of Israel, so that the fish of the sea, the birds of the heavens, the beasts of the field, all creeping things that creep on the earth, and all men who are on the face of the earth shall shake at My presence. The mountains shall be thrown down, the steep places shall fall, and every wall shall fall to the ground." I will call for a

sword against Gog throughout all My mountains,' says the Lord God. 'Every man's sword will be against his brother. And I will bring him to judgment with pestilence and bloodshed; I will rain down on him, on his troops, and on the many peoples who are with him, flooding rain, great hailstones, fire, and brimstone.'

He will cause recriminations among the invaders so that they turn on one another and destroy each other on the battlefield. He will judge the invaders with pestilence and bloodshed and pelt them with flooding rain and great hailstones, fire, and brimstone. He says He will knock the bow out of Gog's left hand and cause the arrows to fall out of his right hand. Gog and his troops will fall on the mountains of Israel. And they shall be prey for the birds of prey of every sort and be devoured by the beasts of the field.

The rout of Gog and his massive army will be so comprehensive and complete that only a sixth of the invading army will be left alive to go and tell their story. For seven months, Israel will be burying the dead to cleanse the land by specially trained, dedicated search parties in the manner that one will handle a nuclear aftermath to avoid radioactive contamination. For seven years, after the invasion, Israel will be feeding off the fuel of the invaders as they plunder those who plundered them. This war will have repercussions far beyond the borders of Israel as God visits His wrath on many nations that participated in it in any capacity.

God's purpose for intervening on Israel's behalf are twofold. First is to make His holy name known among His people, Israel, so Israel will not profane His name any more. After this miraculous intervention, Israel will know that He is the Lord their God from that day forward. God has always intervened in all the wars of Israel with her Islamic enemies. There are untold numbers of miraculous interventions and inexplicable victories in the face of apparent annihilation, but not many in Israel believe this. After this destruction of this massive invading force, well, there will be no more room for doubt about God's divine intervention in the lives of Israel, especially on the battlefield.

Secondly, it is also to let the nations know that He is the the Holy Lord in Israel. God will use this divine intervention to set His glory among the nations when they see His judgement on the invaders. The Gentiles will finally come to realise that Israel went into captivity for her iniquity and their unfaithfulness to their God.

In the Psalm 83 war, God uses the IDF to defend Israel and destroy her enemies, the same way He used the 300 men of Gideon to destroy the Midianites in the book of Judges. But in Ezekiel 38 and 39, we see God Himself intervening on Israel's behalf to destroy her enemies.

After the Psalm 83 total extermination of the inner circle of Israel's Muslim neighbours, for by this divine routing of an overwhelming army made up of Israel's outer ring of Islamic neighbours, one wonders what will be left of Islam and their dream of world conquest and world domination. She will be key in the Antichrist's one world religious system together with apostate Christless Christianity and an array of assorted religions, but they will succumb to the might of Christ Himself at the battle for Jerusalem as part of the wars of Armageddon, never to rise again. And from that time the kingdom of God will fill the whole earth when the kingdoms of this world become the kingdom of our God and of His Christ.

> 'I will set My glory among the nations; all the nations shall see My judgment which I have executed, and My hand which I have laid on them. So the house of Israel shall know that I am the Lord their God from that day forward. The Gentiles shall know that the house of Israel went into captivity for their iniquity; because they were unfaithful to Me, therefore I hid My face from them. I gave them into the hand of their enemies, and they all fell by the sword. According to their uncleanness and according to their transgressions I have dealt with them, and hidden My face from them."'

> 'Therefore thus says the Lord God: "Now I will bring back the captives of Jacob, and have mercy on the

whole house of Israel; and I will be jealous for My holy name—after they have borne their shame, and all their unfaithfulness in which they were unfaithful to Me, when they dwelt safely in their own land and no one made them afraid. When I have brought them back from the peoples and gathered them out of their enemies' lands, and I am hallowed in them in the sight of many nations, 28 then they shall know that I am the Lord their God, who sent them into captivity among the nations, but also brought them back to their land, and left none of them captive any longer. And I will not hide My face from them anymore; for I shall have poured out My Spirit on the house of Israel," says the Lord God.'

(Ezekiel 39:21–29)

Maranatha!

THE BATTLE OF ARMAGEDDON

THE BATTLE OF ARMAGEDDON OR THE BATTLE OF THE GREAT DAY OF GOD ALMIGHTY

Now I saw heaven opened, and behold, a white horse. And He who sat on him was called Faithful and True, and in righteousness He judges and makes war. His eyes were like a flame of fire, and on His head were many crowns. He had a name written that no one knew except Himself. He was clothed with a robe dipped in blood, and His name is called The Word of God. And the armies in heaven, clothed in fine linen, white and clean, followed Him on white horses. Now out of His mouth goes a sharp sword, that with it He should strike the nations. And He Himself will rule them with a rod of iron. He Himself treads the winepress of the fierceness and wrath of Almighty God. And He has on His robe and on His thigh a name written:

> KING OF KINGS AND
> LORD OF LORDS.

The Beast and His Armies Defeated

Then I saw an angel standing in the sun; and he cried with a loud voice, saying to all the birds that fly in the midst of heaven, 'Come and gather together for the supper of the great God, that you may eat the flesh of kings, the flesh of captains, the flesh of mighty men, the flesh of horses and of those who sit on them, and the flesh of all people, free and slave, both small and great.'

And I saw the beast, the kings of the earth, and their armies, gathered together to make war against Him who sat on the horse and against His army. Then the beast was captured, and with him the false prophet who worked signs in his presence, by which he deceived those who received the mark of the beast and those who worshiped his image. These two were cast alive into the lake of fire burning with brimstone. And the rest were killed with the sword which proceeded from the mouth of Him who sat on the horse. And all the birds were filled with their flesh.

This mother of all battles is not really a battle but a series of wars between Christ Jesus and the armies of heaven and the Antichrist and his fiendish forces and the armies of the nations to finally determine who controls the earth—Christ, the King of Kings and Lord of Lords, or the great dragon, that serpent of old (reference to the Garden of Eden) called the devil and Satan, who deceives the whole world. In the first coming of the Jesus, He came as Saviour and the Suffering Servant, preaching peace and giving His life for the salvation of mankind. In His second coming, He is coming with vengeance in His heart to punish and destroy His enemies and those who destroy His earth and oppress His people, the Jews. He is coming as the Warrior King, this time to settle scores:

'For behold, the day is coming,
Burning like an oven,
And all the proud, yes, all who do wickedly will be stubble.
And the day which is coming shall burn them up,'
Says the LORD of hosts,
'That will leave them neither root nor branch.'

(Malachi 4:1)

Isaiah 61:2 says, 'And the day of vengeance of our God.'

Jesus, in His lengthy answer to the disciples' question as to the end of the age and the signs to look for at the time of His second advent (in Matthew 24 and 25), explains when this will happen and that this will be.

Immediately after the tribulation of those days the sun will be darkened, and the moon will not give its light; the stars will fall from heaven, and the powers of the heavens will be shaken. Then the sign of the Son of Man will appear in heaven, and then all the tribes of the earth will mourn, and they will see the Son of Man coming on the clouds of heaven with power and great glory. And He will send His angels with a great sound of a trumpet, and they will gather together His elect from the four winds, from one end of heaven to the other.

(Matthew 24:29–31)

This will happen at the end of the seven-year tribulation. It is His coming and the wars that actually end the tribulation and before the millennium begins. This will be the dramatic conclusion to the times of the Gentiles, when Israel has endured oppression by Gentile nations that began in Egypt and continued with Nebuchadnezzar's Babylonian conquest and exile of the Jews in 606 BC and will continue until the last world empire of the Antichrist, revived Greece.

This war will not be limited to the valley of Megiddo, as popularly assumed, but will actually engulf much of the entire Middle East.

According to Revelation 16:16, Armageddon will be the focal point of these battles, which will be fought in at least four different theatres or campaigns.

> Then the sixth angel poured out his bowl on the great river Euphrates, and its water was dried up, so that the way of the kings from the east might be prepared. And I saw three unclean spirits like frogs coming out of the mouth of the dragon, out of the mouth of the beast, and out of the mouth of the false prophet. For they are spirits of demons, performing signs, which go out to the kings of the earth and of the whole world, to gather them to the battle of that great day of God Almighty.

> 'Behold, I am coming as a thief. Blessed is he who watches, and keeps his garments, lest he walk naked and they see his shame.'

> And they gathered them together to the place called in Hebrew, Armageddon.
> (Revelation 16:12–16)

This valley of Armageddon is said to refer to the valley of Esdraelon, or the valley of Jezreel in northern Israel. This fourteen-mile valley has been the scene of many great battles in the past and will be the scene for one of the final campaigns to determine the fate of this planet. Scripture indicates that this war will be fought over two hundred miles north and south of the holy land and will cover much of Israel.

This campaign will cover at least four battles. During this campaign, Satan will mount one final onslaught on the Jewish nation in his final attempt to exterminate them. He will actually incite his fiendish armies to destroy the holy city of Jerusalem and will come pretty close to achieving that, but Christ will come just in time to rescue the city and His surviving Jewish brethren.

According to Zechariah 12:1–9:

The burden of the Word of the LORD against Israel. Thus says the LORD, who stretches out the heavens, lays the foundation of the earth, and forms the spirit of man within him: 'Behold, I will make Jerusalem a cup of drunkenness to all the surrounding peoples, when they lay siege against Judah and Jerusalem. And it shall happen in that day that I will make Jerusalem a very heavy stone for all peoples; all who would heave it away will surely be cut in pieces, though all nations of the earth are gathered against it. In that day,' says the LORD, 'I will strike every horse with confusion, and its rider with madness; I will open My eyes on the house of Judah, and will strike every horse of the peoples with blindness. And the governors of Judah shall say in their heart, "The inhabitants of Jerusalem are my strength in the LORD of hosts, their God." In that day I will make the governors of Judah like a firepan in the woodpile, and like a fiery torch in the sheaves; they shall devour all the surrounding peoples on the right hand and on the left, but Jerusalem shall be inhabited again in her own place—Jerusalem.

'The LORD will save the tents of Judah first, so that the glory of the house of David and the glory of the inhabitants of Jerusalem shall not become greater than that of Judah. In that day the LORD will defend the inhabitants of Jerusalem; the one who is feeble among them in that day shall be like David, and the house of David shall be like God, like the Angel of the LORD before them. It shall be in that day that I will seek to destroy all the nations that come against Jerusalem.'

It is apparent from the above that God will supernaturally empower the Jews to fight beyond their human abilities. Much of the surrounding nations, Israel's neighbours, who have been thorns and briers in Israel's eyes, will be devoured like stubble because, as always, they will be on the wrong side of the war.

> Then I heard the man clothed in linen, who was above the waters of the river, when he held up his right hand and his left hand to heaven, and swore by Him who lives forever, that it shall be for a time, times, and half a time; and when the power of the holy people has been completely shattered, all these things shall be finished.
>
> (Daniel 12:7)

Jesus will hasten to rescue the Jews when they are finally beaten, when Jerusalem is overrun, and when half the city has fallen to the invading Antichrist fiends.

THE BATTLE OF JEHOSHAPHAT

> 'For behold, in those days and at that time,
> When I bring back the captives of Judah and Jerusalem,
> I will also gather all nations,
> And bring them down to the Valley of Jehoshaphat;
> And I will enter into judgment with them there
> On account of My people, My heritage Israel,
> Whom they have scattered among the nations;
> They have also divided up My land.
> They have cast lots for My people,
> Have given a boy as payment for a harlot,
> And sold a girl for wine, that they may drink.
>
> 'Indeed, what have you to do with Me,
> O Tyre and Sidon, and all the coasts of Philistia?
> Will you retaliate against Me?
> But if you retaliate against Me,

Swiftly and speedily I will return your retaliation upon
your own head.'

(Joel 3:1–4)

God declares in Joel 3 that this will happen at the end of days, when
He will gather all nations to come to Jerusalem to face Him in battle
for their stance against Him and against His city. God rebukes the
Palestinians for claiming the city; they have no connection with it, nor
does their God, Allah. So the Muslim temple on the ruins of the old
temple is an affront to God, and He asks pointedly, 'Moreover, what are
you to Me?' God is saying in Joel that He will use the regathered Jews
as instruments to exact retribution on these enemies. God is rebuking
the Palestinians that they want control of the Temple Mount so that
they can keep it holy. God says, 'I am able to keep My temple holy, and
I don't need you to do that for me because I do not know you, anyway.'
The Palestinian Muslims keep defiling and desecrating the Temple
Mount with their constant rioting and vandalism over the sacred site.

God declares, 'You who want war, I am going to give you war this
time, so come over and let's do battle.'

According to Joel 3:11–14:

Assemble and come, all you nations,
And gather together all around.
Cause Your mighty ones to go down there, O LORD.
'Let the nations be wakened, and come up to the Valley
of Jehoshaphat;
For there I will sit to judge all the surrounding nations.
Put in the sickle, for the harvest is ripe.
Come, go down;
For the winepress is full,
The vats overflow—
For their wickedness *is* great.'
Multitudes, multitudes in the valley of decision!
For the day of the LORD *is* near in the valley of decision.

These people and the nations that support their unholy cause have taunted the Jews and the God of Israel with war and the threat of war for centuries, and now God is calling their bluff: 'Come and let's do battle.' And God says, 'I will draw you into the theatre of war so we can fight.'

The battles grow so fierce that God will deploy His angelic host, led by Michael, the archangel that watches over Israel.

According to Daniel 12:1:

> At that time Michael shall stand up,
> The great prince who stands watch over the sons of
> your people;
> And there shall be a time of trouble,
> Such as never was since there was a nation,
> Even to that time.
> And at that time your people shall be delivered,
> Every one who is found written in the book.

So it is clear that much of these battles would be fought in the heavenlies, between the forces of God and those of Satan. This is the war to end all wars.

THE BATTLE FOR JERUSALEM

As the battle of Jehoshaphat comes to an end, the battle of Jerusalem begins, and it will be one of the most bitterly fought battles. The city will be taken and lost and recaptured a couple of times, but the Antichrist and his forces will have difficulty holding on to the city as God supernaturally intervenes.

According to Zechariah 12:2–6:

> 'Behold, I will make Jerusalem a cup of drunkenness
> to all the surrounding peoples, when they lay siege
> against Judah and Jerusalem. And it shall happen in

that day that I will make Jerusalem a very heavy stone for all peoples; all who would heave it away will surely be cut in pieces, though all nations of the earth are gathered against it. In that day,' says the LORD, 'I will strike every horse with confusion, and its rider with madness; I will open My eyes on the house of Judah, and will strike every horse of the peoples with blindness. And the governors of Judah shall say in their heart, "The inhabitants of Jerusalem are my strength in the LORD of hosts, their God." In that day I will make the governors of Judah like a firepan in the woodpile, and like a fiery torch in the sheaves; they shall devour all the surrounding peoples on the right hand and on the left, but Jerusalem shall be inhabited again in her own place—Jerusalem."

Two-thirds of the inhabitants of Israel will perish in these battles as God purges the nation of Israel of all rebels, and the surviving one third will go into the millennium, finally recognising Jesus Christ as their Messiah and King.

According to Zechariah 12:10:

And I will pour on the house of David and on the inhabitants of Jerusalem the Spirit of grace and supplication; then they will look on Me whom they pierced. Yes, they will mourn for Him as one mourns for his only son, and grieve for Him as one grieves for a firstborn.

God will give the inhabitants of Jerusalem and the Jews as a whole special grace to cry out unto Him to intervene in their hour of dire need. This is the spirit of grace and supplication. You see, God is not just going to show up to deliver them, they have to invite Him. It will take extreme pressure for the Jews to finally call on the God of their fathers and in particular, the Messiah-King, to come to their rescue and the moment they do that, when all their capacity to resist their invaders is completely shattered, they will finally cry out to Him, and then The Lion of the tribe of Judah, the Son of David, their own God-Son will show up to their rescue. By this time two thirds of the Jews would have perished.

> And one will say to him, 'What are these wounds between your arms?' Then he will answer, 'Those with which I was wounded in the house of my friends.'
> (Zechariah 13:6)

When their long-awaited Messiah appears, to their surprise, it would be Jesus of Nazareth, the one they rejected and crucified almost two thousand years ago. They will see the nail wounds on His arms and feet and ask what the wounds mean, and He will reply them, 'These are the wounds I was wounded with in the house of those who love Me.' Even though it is obvious that Jesus still 'agonises' over the rejection He suffered at the hands of His own people, He does not hold it against them, recognising that they did it in ignorance and unbelief. They simply did not recognise Him at His first coming, having been blinded by the law and their own warped expectations. But this time, they will not make that mistake again, and all the surviving Jews will believe in Him (after seeing Him) and be saved as a nation.

> 'And it shall come to pass in all the land,'
> Says the LORD,
> '*That* two-thirds in it shall be cut off *and* die,
> But *one*-third shall be left in it:
> I will bring the *one*-third through the fire,
> Will refine them as silver is refined,
> And test them as gold is tested.
> They will call on My name,
> And I will answer them.
> I will say, "This *is* My people"
> And each one will say, "The LORD *is* my God."'
> (Zechariah 13:8–9)

THE BATTLE OF THE JORDAN VALLEY

The Antichrist will turn his attention on the remnant Jews who had taken shelter in Jordan (Daniel 11:41; Revelation 12:6, 14) to try to destroy them. These have been hidden in Bozra or the ancient city of Petra by God at the beginning of the Antichrist's reign, but now the Antichrist finally sets his sights on them to destroy them too. Here Jesus will fly over Bozra, and they will actually see Him fly over the city as He destroys the forces of the Antichrist and soils His white garment with the blood of the slain. This is real, physical war involving weapons and bloodshed, except that the Lord's weapon is the sword that comes out of His mouth.

According to Joel 2:20, the Antichrist's northern army will suffer heavy losses in Jerusalem and in the valley of Jehoshaphat and retreat to the Jordan valley near the Dead Sea, but this will be God's design to destroy them there. This valley will witness the arrival of the 200,000,000 strong army from the east to confront the Antichrist and his forces, intending to seize the rich oil wells of the Middle East for themselves.

THE BATTLE OF ARMAGEDDON

This will be the site of the final battle that will involve the armies of the world, numbering several hundred millions. In this battle, it appears everybody is fighting everybody, and nuclear weapons are actually used in the ensuing melee, killing multiple millions, and as Joel captures it, 'a fire consumes before them, and behind them a flame burns'.

> And another angel came out from the altar, who had power over fire, and he cried with a loud cry to him who had the sharp sickle, saying, 'Thrust in your sharp sickle and gather the clusters of the vine of the earth, for her grapes are fully ripe.' So the angel thrust his sickle into the earth and gathered the vine of the earth, and threw

it into the great winepress of the wrath of God. And the winepress was trampled outside the city, and blood came out of the winepress, up to the horses' bridles, for one thousand six hundred furlongs.

(Revelation 14:17–20)

This depicts the scene at Armageddon when the Lord destroys all His enemies gathered there to do battle with Him. Can anyone imagine the sheer futility of man in seeking to do battle with the Lord, He whose weapons of warfare are not carnal or natural weapons of guns and bullets but the Word of His mouth? There will be so much death and destruction and bloodshed that beggars description. The blood of the slain at Armageddon will flow waist deep for over two hundred miles.

This will be the scene of much devastation and bloodshed where countless millions will meet their death, signalling the end of Gentile military power, which the devil has used to bring carnage to the world and Israel for millennia, never to rise again.

Then returns Jesus. He would have finished destroying all the enemies of Israel as He finally sets His feet on the Mount of Olives.

Behold, the day of the LORD is coming,
And your spoil will be divided in your midst.
For I will gather all the nations to battle against Jerusalem;
The city shall be taken,
The houses rifled,
And the women ravished.
Half of the city shall go into captivity,
But the remnant of the people shall not be cut off from the city.

Then the LORD will go forth
And fight against those nations,
As He fights in the day of battle.
And in that day His feet will stand on the Mount of Olives,
Which faces Jerusalem on the east.

And the Mount of Olives shall be split in two,
From east to west,
Making a very large valley;
Half of the mountain shall move toward the north
And half of it toward the south.

(Zechariah 14:1–4)

When Christ appears in the sky, all the warring factions will stop fighting each other and train their weapons on the returning Christ in their final bid to stop Him from taking over the earth. And what a futile effort this will be. With the breath of His mouth, He will consume all His enemies in their entirety. The blood of the slain soldiers, mixed with the nuclear fallout, will flow the entire length of the holy land, about two hundred miles.

THE SUPPER OF THE GREAT GOD

Then I saw an angel standing in the sun; and he cried with a loud voice, saying to all the birds that fly in the midst of heaven, 'Come and gather together for the supper of the great God, you may eat the flesh of kings, the flesh of captains, the flesh of mighty men, the flesh of horses and of those who sit on them, and the flesh of all people, free and slave, both small and great.'

And I saw the beast, the kings of the earth, and their armies, gathered together to make war against Him who sat on the horse and against His army. Then the beast was captured, and with him the false prophet who worked signs in his presence, by which he deceived those who received the mark of the beast and those who worshiped his image. These two were cast alive into the lake of fire burning with brimstone. And the rest were killed with the sword which proceeded from the mouth of Him who sat on the horse. And all the birds were filled with their flesh.

(Revelation 19:17–21)

When the battle is over, God will invite the birds of the air and the beasts of the field to supper, to feed on the millions of human carcasses strewn all over the breadth and length of Palestine. Satan's final attempt to resist Jesus' takeover of planet earth and destroy His chosen people will finally be over.

It is clear from several Bible passages that the 'battle of the great day of God Almighty' will consist of at least four battles or campaigns spread over the entire land of Palestine.

1. First, Jesus goes to Edom to rescue Israel from the hand of the Antichrist, where he soils His garment with blood (Isaiah 63:1–6).
2. The Lord then goes to the valley of Megiddo, where He defeats the world's army battling Israel there (Revelation 16:12–16).
3. Then He defeats most of the remaining of the world's army in the valley of Jehoshaphat (Joel 3:1–2, 9–17; Revelation 16:17–21).
4. Finally, He will go to Jerusalem to destroy the returning army of the Antichrist, which is seeking to finally exterminate the Jewish people and destroy the holy city of Jerusalem (Zechariah 12:1–9; Revelation 16:17–21).

THE MAIN PROTAGONISTS AT ARMAGEDDON

Many of the armies of the nations of the world would be involved in the final series of battles that have to be known as the battle of Armageddon. The Antichrist is the king of the north, and therefore, his army is the northern army (Joel 2:20). The northern power base consists of Turkey, Syria, Iraq, Iran, and Lebanon. According to Daniel 11:40, his northern army defeats the king of the south. The southern power base consists of Egypt, Sudan, and Libya. So these will form the nucleus of his army to start with. Thus, this will be his revised Roman Empire, which he gains control over in the middle of the week, but over time, he will form his own empire, which is revived Greece, and conquer many nations to bolster his fighting force. Add to this all the nations that the three froglike spirits go out to gather to join him in battle (Revelation 16:16).

Then there are the armies from the east and the north which primarily join in the fray to fight the Antichrist. These may well be the two hundred million Oriental army from the East and the northern European countries that rebel against his increasingly draconian rule and send an army to do battle with him (Daniel 11:41–44).

It is inconceivable that America and the West do not feature anywhere in these wars. Daniel 11:39 say, 'He shall act against the strongest fortresses.' These strong fortresses may well refer to an alliance of Western nations, which are arguably the strongest fortresses. These may enter the war on the side of Israel initially when the Antichrist goes against the holy land. Micah 5:5–6 says that when the Assyrian (another name for the Antichrist) enters our land, they will raise against him seven shepherds and eight princely men to defend the land. These may be the Western allies that God will initially deploy to defend Israel and Jerusalem.

Then of course, there is the IDF, who will fight like angelic beings (Zechariah 12:6, 8; 14:14).

The one thing that is clear is that all these warring factions will fight one another till Christ appears in the sky. Then they will put aside their differences and unite in their opposition against Him and be destroyed by Him as a result.

Thus on the day Christ returns to the earth, He will destroy all His enemies, all in one day; liberate Jerusalem and the Jewish people; bind Satan and shut him up in the bottomless pit for a thousand years; kill the Antichrist with the breath of His mouth; capture the false prophet and the beast from the bottomless pit; and cast them alive into the lake of fire, where they will be tormented forever and ever.

Satan's rebellious career is finally over, and Revelation 11:15 comes to pass:

> Seventh Trumpet: **Then the** seventh angel sounded: And **the**re were loud voices in heaven, saying, '**The kingdoms of this world** have become **the kingdoms of** our Lord and **of** His Christ, and He shall reign forever and ever!'

And Daniel 2:34–35 is fulfilled:

> You watched while a stone was cut out without hands, which struck the image on its feet of iron and clay, and broke them in pieces. Then the iron, the clay, the bronze, the silver, and the gold were crushed together, and became like chaff from the summer threshing floors; the wind carried them away so that no trace of them was found. And the stone that struck the image became a great mountain and filled the whole earth.

Finally, the times of the Gentiles—where Satan has used the Gentile nations to resist the purposes and plans of God for the earth and to persecute and attempt to destroy God's chosen people, the Jews, and to take God's land and His city for themselves—finally comes to an abrupt end. Israel has been through a lot since the time God called their fathers to set them aside for Himself, but in the end, it will all be worth it when God finally fulfils His promises to their fathers and establishes them as the wealthiest and the greatest nation on planet earth with David, the king, as their king forever.

Maranatha.

DANIEL'S SEVENTIETH WEEK AND THE TRIBULATION (DANIEL 9:24–27)

INTRODUCTION

King Nebuchadnezzar conquered Israel and Jerusalem in 606 BC and took some royal captives to Babylon to serve at the king's court, among whom was Daniel. He was a very godly young man with an incredible prophetic gift. In 538 BC, after living in Babylon for almost 7 decades, he read the prophet Jeremiah's prophecy in Jeremiah 25:11, which declared that 'this whole land shall be a desolation, and an astonishment, and these nations shall serve the king of Babylon seventy years'. He understood that the Babylonian captivity would last 70 years. He realised that the 70 years should end in 2 years in 536 BC.

So Daniel began to pray and to intercede for his nation and to ask God to reveal to him the future of the Jewish people (Daniel 9:1–3). God answered him by sending the angel Gabriel to give him 'skill and understanding' about the future of the Jewish nation. Daniel's vision of 'seventy weeks of years' revealed to him the precise day when Israel will reject and 'cut off' their Messiah and almost 2,000 years to the Messiah's Second Coming to set up His everlasting kingdom on earth (Daniel 9:24–27).

Daniel's vision spoke of a total of 'seventy sevens' or 'seventy weeks of years', equalling 490 biblical years. The biblical solar lunar year has 360 days, not our 365-day lunar year, and a biblical month is 30 days. In the book of Revelation, John calculates the last part of the tribulation from the abomination of desolation (when the Antichrist would enter the Holy of Holies in the Jewish temple and set up his image and demand that the Jews worship him as a god) to the end of the tribulation, the day Christ descends from heaven as three and a half years or 1,260 days or 42 months (Revelation 13:14–15).

The expression 70 weeks literally means '70 sevens of years'. We know from scripture that the last week (9:27) is made up of two parts of three and a half years each (Daniel 7:25, 12:7; Revelation 11:2, 3; 12:5, 14; 13:5). The whole period of 7 sevens is 490 years, which are determined or marked off concerning His people, Israel, and the holy city of Jerusalem.

Six events are to take place during these 490 years relative to Israel and Jerusalem for 6 purposes (Daniel 6:10; 9:1–23):

1. *To finish the transgression.* Israel will finish her rebellion against God (Galatians 3:17–25; Luke 19:37–44). Israel was broken off God's agenda for rejecting their Messiah (Romans 11:20, 25–29; Isaiah 66:77–10; Matthew 23, 37–39; Luke 19:28–44).

2. *To make an end of sins.* The end of Israel's sins will not come until after the tribulation, from which time Israel will obey God forever (Ezekiel 36:24–30, 37:24–27; Zechariah 14:1–24).

3. *To make reconciliation (atonement) for iniquity.* Israel has not yet appropriated her part of the atonement Christ made for the whole world. She will do this at the return of Christ (Zechariah 13:1–7; Romans 11:25–27).

4. *To bring in everlasting righteousness.* After finishing her transgression, end of sins made, full benefits of the atonement are realised by Israel. Then everlasting righteousness will be ushered in (Isaiah 9:6–7, 12:1–6; Daniel 7:13, 14, 18, 27; Matthew 25:31–46).

5. *To seal up the vision and prophecy.* That is to make an end of vision and prophecy or prophet. There will be no need for

prophets to rebuke Israel anymore, 'for all shall know the Lord from the least of them to the greatest' (Hebrews 8:11).

6. *To anoint the most holy.* The holy of holies will be cleansed from the abomination of desolation and the sacrilege of Gentiles and the establishment of the Millennial Temple (Revelation 11:2).

These are the 3 divisions of the 70 weeks (490 years):

1. In the 1st period of 7 sevens, or 49 years, the holy city, street, and wall were to be rebuilt, even in troublesome times (Daniel 9:27). This began with the command to restore and build Jerusalem unto the Messiah (Nehemiah 2:1–6; Daniel 9:25–26). The command was given on 14 March 445 BC by King Artaxerxes, Babylon.

2. The 2nd period consisted of 62 sevens, or 434 years. It began immediately after the first period of the 7 sevens, or 49 years, and continued without a break to the time when the Messiah was cut off or crucified on 6 April AD 32 (Luke 19:28–44; Matthew 23:37–39; Daniel 9:26). Thus, 49 + 434 = 483 years from the third decree to the crucifixion of the Messiah, or 69 years of the 70 sevens of years, leaving the last period of 7 years concerning Israel and Jerusalem to be fulfilled after the crucifixion.

3. The 3rd period will consist of one 7-year period, better known as the tribulation or Daniel's 70th week. The crucifixion of the Messiah ended the 69th week, and God stopped/suspended his prophetic time clock and His dealings with Israel as a nation. They were broken off in unbelief and their city destroyed, as foretold in AD 70 by the Romans (Daniel 9:26; Matthew 21:43, 23:37–39, 24:2; Luke 21:20–24; Matthew 23:37–39; Luke 13:34–35).

The 70th week will be the last 7 years of this dispensation and will parallel the 7-year covenant between the Antichrist and Israel (Daniel 9:27). It will be the time when all the events of Revelation 6:1–19:21

will be fulfilled and the whole tribulation runs its course. The events of this week were revealed to John in detail but not to Daniel. This week of years will begin after the rapture of the church and end at the Second Coming of Christ. Between the 69th and the 70th week during the time of Israel's rejection of their Messiah is when the present church age comes in.

ISRAEL'S TIME OF VISITATION

On this day, 6 April AD 32, Jesus entered Jerusalem on a foal, and the multitudes of disciples praised God and hailed Him, saying:

> 'Blessed is the King who comes in the name of the Lord! Peace in heaven and glory in the highest.'

> And some of the Pharisees called Him from the crowd, **'Teacher, rebuke your disciples'.** But He answered and said to them, **'I tell you that if these should keep silent, the stones would immediately cry out.'**
> (Luke 19:28–44)

That was the day of decision for Israel to accept or reject Jesus as their promised Messiah-King, and the nation's political and religious leaders rejected Him. Five days after rejecting Him, they crucified Him. And God postponed His promised kingdom for Israel. Less than forty years later, in AD 70, the Roman army razed Jerusalem to the ground, killing over one million of them in fulfilment of Christ's prophecy in Luke 19:44 and in tragic fulfilment of their own bone-chilling pronouncements in Matthew 27:23, 'Let Him be crucified', and Matthew 27:25, 'His blood be on us and on our children'.

Thus in AD 70, God judged and finished with Judaism, with its temple destroyed and the priesthood scattered. He was finished with Judaism forever and Jesus Christ became the head and founder of the Christian church, composed of believing Jews and Gentiles, elected by

His grace. Thus Israel missed their time of visitation in the same way they could not enter the promised land of Canaan to take possession because of unbelief and had to wander in the wilderness for forty years till a new generation was raised to enter and possess the land.

Daniel 9:26b says, 'And till the end of the war desolations are determined.' Sadly, until the Messiah comes to liberate Israel at Armageddon, Israel has faced one war after another, and it has seen desolations throughout her history. And it is all because she missed her time of visitation.

Only that this time, Israel have had to wait almost 2,000 years now to possess the kingdom promised to their fathers. In the period between the end of the 69th week and the 70th week, God has raised the church, made of Jews and Gentiles, to witness to all the world with His offer of salvation to those who would believe in His Son, Jesus Christ, as Lord and Saviour. During the final 70th week, His attention once again will focus on the Jewish people to finish the 490 years He set aside for them. During this period, when the church is raptured to heaven, He will once again use the Jewish people as His main witness to the world in the form of the 144,000 Jewish evangelists.

See how after rejecting their Messiah, God's attention shifts from the Jews to the Gentile world. Paul, in Acts 28:28, after meeting with the Jewish leaders in Rome, declared, 'Therefore let it be known to you that the salvation of God has been sent to the Gentiles, and they will hear it' (Matthew 21:33–43; Acts 9:15, 13:45–47, 26:17–18). Yes, He is still the God of Israel, but His focus is clearly on His bride, the Gentile–Jewish church. However, with the approach of the end of the age, it is clear that God is slowly but certainly turning to His ancient covenant people the Jews (Isaiah 11:12). God has not broken His promise to Israel, but these are unrealised or postponed because of their unbelief and disobedience.

THE TRIBULATION

The tribulation will begin to affect Israel before the seventieth week begins. When the Antichrist arises at the beginning of the week, Israel will be undergoing persecution by the whore (Revelation 17) and the ten kings of revised Rome (Daniel 9:27). That is why a seven-year peace treaty will seem so attractive to Israel in the first place. But it will be a covenant with death (Isaiah 28:18).

The Divisions of the Tribulation

The first division is the first three and a half years of the seventieth week, known as the lesser tribulation, because the persecution is not as intense as the last three and a half years. Israel's persecution this time will come from the whore and the ten kings of revised Rome. It covers Revelation 6:1–9:21. The judgements of the sixth seal and the first six trumpets come in this period, proving there is tribulation.

The last division, the great tribulation, takes place in the last three and a half years of the week. It is called the great tribulation because the persecution of Israel is more intense. The Antichrist, who will protect Israel for the first three and a half years, will break his covenant with them in the middle of the week and become her most bitter enemy and try to destroy her when the Jews refuse to worship him. This is what calls for God's judgement of the seven vials of the last three and a half years (Revelation 10:1–19:21). This is Israel's worse trouble than any time in her history. That is why it is known as the time of Jacob's trouble. May God have mercy on our brothers and sisters, the Jewish people.

The Purpose of the Tribulation

1. to purify Israel and bring them back to a place where God can fulfil the everlasting covenants He made with their fathers (Isaiah 2:6, 3:26, 16:1–5, 24:1–23, 26:20–21; Ezekiel 20:33–34, 22:17–22; Romans 11:25–29)

2. to purify Israel of all rebels (Ezekiel 20:33–34; Zechariah 13:8–9; Malachi 3:3–4)

3. to plead with and bring Israel into the bond of the new covenant (Ezekiel 20:33–34, 36:24–28; Malachi 4:3–4)

4. to judge Israel and to punish them for their rejection of the Messiah and to make them willing to accept Him when He comes a second time (Ezekiel 20:33–34; Zechariah 12:9–13, 14:1–15; Matthew 24:15–31)

5. to judge the nations for their persecution of Israel (Isaiah 63:1–5; Joel 3; Revelation 6:1–19, 21)

6. to bring Israel to complete repentance (Zechariah 12:9–13; Romans 11:26–29; Matthew 23:39)

7. to fulfil the things of Daniel 9:24–27; Revelation 6:1–19, 21; Matthew 24:15, 29

8. to cause Israel to flee to the wilderness of Edom and Moab and to be so persecuted by the nations that they will have to turn to God for help (Isaiah 16:1–5; Ezekiel 20:33–35; Daniel 11:40, 12:7; Hosea 2:14–17; Matthew 24:15–21; Revelation 12)

THE DAY OF THE LORD WILL COME AS A THIEF IN THE NIGHT

It is generally believed that nobody will know the time or day of the rapture, not even believers, because the Lord Jesus said even He did not know while He was on the earth. We want to take a much closer look at the whole council of God on this issue. In my last write-up on the crucial subject of the rapture, we learnt that:

- It was a New Testament doctrine revealed to the apostle Paul (1 Corinthians 15:51–58).
- Unlike the Second Coming of the Lord, the rapture is a 'signless' event.
- It will take the world by surprise (Matthew 24:36).
- It would be an electrifyingly sudden event (1 Corinthians 15:52). It will all be over in a nanosecond.
- It will be a selective event, only for those who are in Christ (1 Thessalonians 4:13).
- And it will be a spectacular event, preceded by a shout, the voice of the archangel, and a trumpet blast (1 Thessalonians 4:16).

In this article, we are going to learn that the rapture is not going to take watchful believers by surprise as any Christian who is active on the prophetic circuit even today should be living in a heightened expectation of the rapture in his/her lifetime.

Yes, in Matthew 24:36, Jesus reportedly said, 'But of that day and hour, no one knows, not even the angels of heaven, but My Father only.'

In fact, He said in Mark 13:32, 'But of that day and hour no one knows, not even the angels in heaven, nor the Son, but only the Father.'

If you will remember, not long ago, we discussed the fact that when we come to consider the person of Jesus, we have to be aware that there are times He speaks with exclusive reference to His humanity. In those instances, He may subordinate Himself to the Father and will focus on His human weakness, dependence on the Father and His human limitations. These do not detract from His omnipotence or omniscience or omnipresence as God. So when He says 'I of Myself can do nothing', He means as a human being.

There are other times He speaks exclusively as God, all-powerful and all-knowing, but this does not do away with His humanity, being subject to human weaknesses, such as you and I are. For instance, He had to be anointed by God for ministry (Luke 4:14, 18–19; Acts 10:38).

In the above scriptures (Matthew 24:36; Mark 13:32), where Jesus clearly, unequivocally says He did not know the time of His return to earth, I would like to submit to you that that is not the whole story. For Jesus to be fully God, which we believe He is, He has to be eternal, omnipotent, omnipresent, and also *omniscient*, which means all-knowing. If there was one iota of fact hidden from Jesus Christ, then we cannot say He is God. But we know He is God. He is our Lord and our God (John 20:28). In the accounts above, Jesus was speaking exclusively as a human being. The Godhead has always acted in concert (together). When it comes to God, it has always been 'let us' (Genesis 1:26). While it may have been true that Jesus in his humanity may not have known when He was due back on earth to take His bride home, the Lord Jesus Christ, the omniscient God, has always known all things, including the time of the rapture of His church to be with Him in heaven.

THE RAPTURE WILL NOT COME AS A THIEF
IN THE NIGHT FOR WATCHFUL BELIEVERS

In 1 Thessalonians 5:1–11, the apostle Paul addresses two groups of people regarding the day of the Lord. Obviously, he is addressing believers here as are all the epistles, but he addresses others, non-believers, as well.

Note the flow of thought here:

In verse 1 he writes, 'You have no need that I should write to you.' In verse 2, he continues, 'For you yourselves know.'

In verse 4, he continues, 'But you, brethren' (or brothers and sisters). And he ends it with 'should overtake you as a thief'.

In verse 5, he writes, 'You are all sons of the light . . . We are not . . .' Here he includes himself as a fellow believer. In verse 6, he continues, 'Let us not sleep . . . but let us watch.' This is continued in all the verses down to 11.

By way of contrast, he talks about the unbelieving world differently.

He starts with verse 3: 'They say . . . comes upon them . . . and they shall not escape.' In verse 6, he calls them 'others'.

This is verse 7: 'Those who sleep . . . those who get drunk. They are sons of the night and of the darkness.' They are appointed to the wrath of God.

So it is clear the great apostle is drawing a contrast here—that the same event will impact the two groups of people differently. First of all, we have said that the rapture would be an exclusive event for those who have trusted Christ for their salvation and are in right standing with Him. In that sense, it has nothing to do with the unbelieving world. But the rapture will be the event that ends this present dispensation and also usher in the day of the Lord or the seven-year tribulation, which has everything to do with Israel and the world.

The Lord is saying we shall know clearly when that day is drawing near because we are not in darkness but we are sons of light. When you are in the light, nothing can be hidden from your sight. As we continue to pore over the light of His Word, He continues to shed fresh light on His agenda for His children every day. We are not of those that sleep, but we are wide awake, watchful, and sober. *Awake* smacks of activeness, *watchful* speaks of alertness and expectation, and *sober* connotes a clear, wide-open mind/eye. In all this, we live in faith or believe in Him and His Word of promise that we are not appointed to wrath or tribulation but that we expect to be rescued any moment, and we go about His work of labouring for souls out of love for Him and for humanity. The keyword for us here is *watchfulness*. Watchful people live in expectation and constant anticipation. They are in a state of preparedness, like the military at boot camps, who sleep with their boots on, ready for any sudden eventuality in the middle of the night. Matthew 25 is a passage about events of His Second Coming, the five virgins lost their place at the wedding feast because they were not watchful. It is not about being filled with the Holy Spirit or any such speculative interpretation. They were not watchful. Unwatchful believers live casually, taking unnecessary risks in life. They've been deceived into thinking that they have time to put their lives in order someday and lured into thinking some sins don't matter.

I am amazed about the many visions and visitations of heaven and hell the Lord has been giving His children lately. And the great majority are authentic visions. All these are the Lord's warnings to His children to get ready for take-off. The wise believer will not only take notice but adjust their lives accordingly. Obviously, there are always five foolish virgins in any ten. Some will be scoffers, like Peter said in 2 Peter 3:4: 'Where is the promise of His coming? For since the fathers fell asleep, all things continue as they were from the beginning of creation.' They fail to notice the changes in the spiritual climate of our day. The doctrine of imminence is more imminent than ever before.

To the unbelieving world, it is life as usual, putting their trust in a false (UN-brokered) peace and economic prosperity. They are creatures of the night and of darkness and are fast asleep. In the night, it is easy for all kinds of creepy creatures to creep upon them. In the night, their eyes are closed in slumber, and they are drowsy and vulnerable. Not only are they asleep, but they are also drunk at night in their life of wanton dissipation and hedonistic carousing. And the Bible says. 'And they shall not escape.' They will have no place to run to when the rapture is over but will have to endure the tribulation and their Antichrist king and his evil mark and constant wars and bloodshed and carnage all over the world. To them, the Lord will surely come as a thief in the night. Do you remember that it was in the night that the enemy came and sowed tares in the farmer's field in Matthew 13:26?

The day of the Lord, which begins with the rapture, includes several key events, (i.e. Joel 2–3; Zechariah 12:2–10, 14; Malachi 4:1; Mark 13; Amos 5:16–20; Isaiah 13; Matthew 24–25):

- the Second Coming of the Lord and the battle of Armageddon to destroy the Antichrist and his army (2 Thessalonians 2:8)
- the battle to liberate Jerusalem and restore Israel to their promised inheritance (Zechariah 8:7, 10:9–10, 12, 14; Ezekiel 36:24)
- the judgement of the nations (Matthew 25:31–46; Joel 3:1–3, 12)
- the entire seven-year tribulation and the terrible reign of the Antichrist, which is wars and many wars, for the Antichrist is a man of war and death (Daniel 7:21, 11:40–45, 8:24–25; Revelation 6:2, 16:13–14; Micah 5:5–6)
- the mass slaughter of tribulation believers and Jews (Daniel 7:21; Revelation 11:7, 13:7, 17:6, 18:24), God's vengeance on sinners and persecutors of Israel
- the renovation of the earth for the millennial reign of Christ to begin on earth.

You can accept Jesus as your Lord and Saviour by saying this simple prayer and by believing in Him in your heart: 'Lord Jesus, I acknowledge that I am a sinner. I believe you are the Son of God and that you died on the cross for my sins. I now invite you into my heart to be my Lord and Saviour. Thank you for saving my soul. Amen' (Romans 10:9–11, 13).

Are you a Christian? Then be assured of your salvation. Go on to develop an intimate relationship with the Lord. It is all about getting to know Jesus through spending time with Him in the Word of God and through prayer. Remember, God *will not admit any stranger* into His heavenly abode. Make sure you confess and repent of all known sins. Don't ignore the destructive power of sin. It could wreck your eternal destiny, so don't play with sin or entertain it in any shape or form in your life. Yes, God does not demand perfection from any of us because it is unattainable on this side of eternity. But that is not the same as ignoring known sin to fester in your life.

Second Corinthians 13:5 says, 'Examine yourself as to whether you are in the faith. Test yourselves. Do you not know yourselves, that Jesus Christ is in you?—unless indeed you are disqualified.' Do not focus on the Antichrist and his mark but rather on living for Christ, because that is how you escape the Antichrist and his mark.

THE RAPTURE: THE BELIEVER'S BLESSED HOPE

The rapture is a New Testament doctrine revealed to the apostle Paul in 1 Corinthians 15:51–58. It is called the coming of the Lord but not the Second Coming of the Lord, which is a different event separated by several years. The word *rapture* is from the Greek word *harpazo*, which means 'to be caught up' or 'to seize suddenly' or 'to snatch away'. The Latin word is *rapio.*

During the rapture, the Lord Jesus will appear in the clouds or the earth's atmosphere with the souls of all dead believers from the time of Adam and Eve and the church age till the time of the rapture. The bodies of the dead saints will be resurrected first to go up and unite with their souls, and the living saints will also be caught up to be with the Lord in the air (1 Thessalonians 4:17). They will all receive glorified bodies like the Lord's (1 John 3:3; 1 Corinthians 15:49), and the Lord Jesus will take them with Him to heaven to the Father.

It is the translation of living believers to heaven without experiencing death in a moment of time. So during the rapture, the Lord Jesus comes down from heaven to the sky, where we meet Him and He takes us to heaven. We do not come back to the earth then. But during the Second Coming, Jesus will return from heaven to the earth with all the multitude of believers to rule and reign on the earth from Jerusalem.

At the Second Coming, Jesus and His troops come to fight the battle of Armageddon, destroy the Antichrist and his world army, bind the devil and put him in the bottomless pit for 1,000 years, liberate the nation of Israel and fulfil all of God's promises to their fathers, judge the nations (sheep and goats, depending on how they have treated Israel in the tribulation (Matthew 25:31–46)), etc. So it is obvious that the rapture and the Second Coming of the Lord are two separate events separated by at least seven years.

KEY SCRIPTURE ON THE RAPTURE

These include 1 Thessalonians 4:15–17; 2 Thessalonians 1:10; Revelation 14:14–16; Matthew 24:31; Titus 2:13; Isaiah 26:20.

In John 14:1–3, Jesus spoke of the rapture, and He said He will come and take us home to be with Him in heaven.

Even though the revelation of the doctrine of the rapture was given to the apostle Paul in the New Testament, there have been raptures all through the Bible, both in the Old Testament and New Testament. Here are the key examples:

1. Enoch in Genesis 5:24.
2. Elijah in 2 Kings 2:11. Enoch and Elijah will be the two witnesses of Revelation 11.
3. The Lord Jesus Christ (1 Corinthians 15:20; Acts 1:9–11; John 20:17).
4. The Old Testament patriarchs were raised at the resurrection of the Lord (Matthew 27:52–53; Ephesians 4:8).
5. The Old Testament and the church saints, dead and alive, that will take place during the first resurrection, when the Lord appears in the air to take them home 1 Thessalonians 4:13–18; 2 Thessalonians 2:1. This is only the first of a series of raptures during the first resurrection (Revelation 20:5–6). This is believed to happen in Revelation 4:1, just before the seven-year tribulation on earth. It is after the rapture of the church that the Antichrist is revealed.
6. Included in the first resurrection, in order, are:

a) the rapture of the 144,000 Jewish evangelist God raises up to evangelise the world after the church is removed from the earth (Revelation 7:1–3, 12:5, 14:1–5)
b) the rapture of the great multitude of tribulation saints, those who come to faith after the rapture and martyred during the tribulation (Revelation 6:9–11, 7:9–17, 15:2–4, 20:4)
c) The rapture of the two (prophets) witnesses after they are killed by the Antichrist (Revelation 11:3–13).

This is the order of the series of raptures that form the first resurrection. This is what Paul meant by *everyone* in his own order in 1 Corinthians 15:20–23.

God always provides an escape for His people before destruction, and this will be no different during the tribulation.

> Be always on the watch, and pray that you may be able
> to escape all that is about to happen, and that you may
> be able to stand before the Son of Man.
>
> (Luke 21:36, NIV)

In Genesis 18:25, when Lot 'haggled' with God over the destruction of Sodom and Gomorrah, Abraham said to God, 'Far be it from You to do such a thing as this, to slay the righteous with the wicked, so that the righteous should be as the wicked: far be it from You! Shall not the Judge of all the earth do right?' God's answer to Abraham seems to suggest that He agreed with Abraham that it was not right to destroy the righteous with the wicked, and He proceeded to deliver righteous Lot and his family out of Sodom before destroying the city and its inhabitants. That principle of always rescuing the righteous first has always applied in every situation where God has had to bring judgement.

When Lot dillydallied and requested to escape to Zoar, the angel told him, 'Hurry, escape there. For I cannot do anything until you arrive there' (Genesis 19:22). The same principle will apply—rapture before tribulation.

- Noah and his family escaped the flood (Hebrews 11:7).
- Lot and his family escaped the fires of Sodom and Gomorrah (2 Peter 2:7–9).
- Israel escaped Egypt (Exodus 12).
- Rahab escaped the destruction of Jericho when she received the Israeli spies to the land (Hebrews 11:31).
- The believers escaped the destruction of Jerusalem in AD 70 (Luke 21:21).
- The believing Jews will escape the tribulation and the onslaught of the Antichrist to Jordan (Daniel 11:4; Revelation 7:3).

This is not going to be any different during the coming tribulation. Listen to the testimony of scripture in Isaiah 26:20–21 (NIV):

> Go, my people, enter your rooms and shut the doors behind you; hide yourselves for a little while until his wrath has passed by. See, the Lord is coming out of his dwelling to punish the people of the earth for their sins. The earth will disclose the blood shed on it; the earth will conceal its slain no longer.

This is a clear escape from the coming tribulation even though it may well refer to Jewish believers taken out of the Antichrist's way. It has been argued that the first resurrection only happens at the end of the tribulation, so believers must have been through the tribulation. But Revelation 20 is clearly a roll call of all the believers who had made it so far to heaven. Don't forget that different companies of believers are raptured to heaven at different times. The Old Testament saints and New Testament believers are raptured before the tribulation begins in Revelation 4:1–2, when the apostle John is summoned to 'come up here' to heaven. These are later seen singing a new song in praise to God before His throne in *Revelation 5:9*, saying, 'For you were slain, And have redeemed us to God by Your blood Out of every tribe and tongue and people and nation.' So it is clear these are not the just the 24 elders before the throne, who are all Jewish. These are redeemed from every nation. Of course, the 144,000 Jewish evangelists and the tribulation saints go through part or all of the tribulation. This is what Paul meant by *everyone* in his own order in 1 Corinthians 15:20–2.

DIFFERENCES BETWEEN THE RAPTURE AND THE SECOND COMING OF CHRIST

1. The rapture is purely a New Testament doctrine, but the Second Coming is a chief Old Testament theme.
2. The rapture and the Second Coming are separated by several years, so they are not the same event.
3. At the rapture, Christ meets the saints in the air and takes them back to heaven with Him to the Father where they will be during the entire period of the tribulation on earth. While in heaven, the saints are judged, given their rewards, and partake of the marriage supper of the Lamb.
4. At the Second Coming, the Lord and the saints, with the armies of heaven, return from heaven to the earth together at the end of the tribulation.
5. The rapture may occur at any moment (imminent), while there are several prophecies to be fulfilled before the second advent can take place. Imminence means it can happen at any time, without any precondition. This is why believers in any age have lived in expectation of the rapture in their lifetime, and rightly so. We are constantly to be looking for the appearance of Christ, not the Antichrist (1 Corinthians 15:51; 1 Thessalonians 4:15; James 5:8; 1 Thessalonians 1:10; 1 Corinthians 1:7; Philippians 3:2).
6. At the rapture, the believers get removed from the earth and are taken to heaven, while at the Second Coming, unbelievers are judged and gets removed from the earth and are sent into the lake of fire.
7. At the rapture, believers are given new glorified bodies, which cannot die again. There is no such bodies for the believers on

earth at the Second Coming, but their bodies remain natural but immortal and can live forever when they eat of the tree of life. These immortal humans can marry and repopulate the earth, while those raptured become like the angels, never marrying and not needing to eat to sustain their lives, even though they can and would eat.

THE NATURE OF THE RAPTURE

1. The rapture is a sign-less event. Nothing has to happen before the rapture. It means it can take place at any time. It is imminent. In fact, the books to the Thessalonians were written to assure them that the rapture had not happened yet, as they were expecting it in their day, as we are.

2. It is a surprise event. It will take the world by surprise. The world will wake up to discover that millions of believers have just vanished (Matthew 24:36). This is not true for believers, though 1 Thessalonians 5:4 says, 'But you brethren are not in darkness, so that this day should overtake you as a thief.'

3. The rapture will be an electrifyingly sudden event. It will all happen in less than a nanosecond and then it's over—according to 1 Corinthians 15:52, 'in a moment, in the twinkling of an eye'. Pilots and crew will disappear in mid-air; drivers will disappear from vehicles and trains; you will stretch your hand to shake hands with your pal, and it will hit thin air; a man will turn over to touch his wife in bed and hit bed linen; a baby will be sucking its mum's milk, and the mum will be clutching empty linen. One cannot imagine the confusion and bewilderment that will descend on the earth and its people. There will be no time to change your mind, so give your life to Christ before it is too late.

4. The rapture is a selective event because only those 'in Christ' shall be taken (1 Thessalonians 4:13; Revelation 3:19; 1

Thessalonians 5:9). This means the rapture is for those who are 'walking in the light, as He is in the light'.

5. In Luke 21:34–36, we have Jesus' promise that some will be 'accounted worthy to escape all these things [pictured in Matthew 24:4–26 and Luke 21:5–19] that shall come to pass and to stand before the Son of man'.

6. The rapture will be a spectacular event. According to 1 Thessalonians 4:16: 'For the Lord will descend from heaven with a shout [a command to all believers to rise from the grave, like He did at Lazarus's tomb], with the voice of the archangel [for protection and safe passage through the air], and with the trumpet of God [a sound of victory and celebration].'

THE SEQUENCE OF EVENTS DURING THE RAPTURE

a) Jesus comes from heaven to the earth's atmosphere with the souls of those who are asleep in the Lord (1 Thessalonians 4:14).

b) In the resurrection, the bodies of those who sleep in the Lord are resurrected from their 'graves' and caught away and reunited with their souls, glorified. Remember that death is only a separation of soul (and spirit) from the body.

c) In the redemption, those of us who are alive and remain will also be taken up and receive glorified bodies. This is the redemption of our bodies (Romans 8:23; 1 Thessalonians 4:15; Philippians 3:21). This glorified body is going to be just like that of the Lord Jesus Christ. This is when our salvation would be complete or perfected. We are saved, we are being saved, and we shall be saved when we have received our glorified bodies (1 John 3:2; Romans 8:29–30).

d) The rapture is a strengthening event; it brings consolation, comfort, and a sense of expectation, which leads to consecrated living and a zeal for soul-winning and evangelism.

e) Every redeemed company of believers has its own unique song of worship to God and the Lamb that nobody else knows, and it reflects their unique salvation experience. The OT saints and the church saints raptured in Revelation 4:1–2 sing in Revelation

5:9–10. The 144,000 Jewish evangelists raptured in the middle of the tribulation sing their unique song in worship to the Lamb in Revelation 14:3, and the multitude of tribulation saints raptured at the end of the tribulation sing the song of Moses and the song of the Lamb in worship of God and the Lamb in Revelation 15:3–4.

The rapture takes place at the end of the church age (period of grace) and begins the seven-year tribulation on earth. It takes place in Revelation 4:1, where the apostle John is summoned to come up to heaven. He is a picture of the church because in Revelations 4–5, we see scenes in heaven with the twenty-four elders (the twelve patriarchs from the OT and the twelve apostles) before the throne of God.

After the rapture, there is a marked change in God's attitude towards humans on earth in general, from mercy (Revelation 1–3) to that of judgement (Revelation 6–19). From the inauguration of the church to the rapture is a period of extended mercy and grace, without judgements, but from the rapture up to and including the Second Coming is a period of judgements and wrath. This is why wicked humanity is seemingly getting away with unspeakable atrocities and wickedness. It is because of God's extended mercy and grace. But judgement will follow soon at some point.

Never are the words *church* or *churches* mentioned ever again after Revelation 3:22 until Revelation 22:6–21. This shows that the church is not on the earth at this time. This warning, 'He who has an ear, let him hear what the Spirit says' to the churches is repeated in Revelation 2:7, 11, 17, 29; 3:6, 13, 22 when the church is still believed to be on the earth. But in Revelation 13:9, when the same warning is issued, it says, 'If anyone has an ear, let him hear.' This is explained by the fact that by this time the church is not on the earth any longer, having already been raptured to heaven.

We do not see any earmarks or features of the church from Revelation 4–19, but rather evidence of Israel is present everywhere. This shows that Israel is the one being dealt with at this time. The Hebrew character of the book is seen everywhere. The enthroned elders in Revelation 4–5 represent the raptured saints, and they are always seen in heaven after

Revelation 4:1. Israel is not mentioned in all of Revelation 1–3, but from Revelation 6–19, the church is not mentioned, and we see Israel centre stage. This shows that the two institutions are being dealt with at different times in the book: the church from Revelation 1–3 and Israel from Revelation 6–19. Revelation 6–19 has a striking resemblance to the Old Testament. Matthew quotes the Old Testament about 92 times, Hebrews about 102 times. But Revelation 6–19 quotes the Old Testament 285 times, showing the close relationship with the Old Testament and Israel. The word *lamb* is used 27 times in Revelation 6–19 but not once in Revelation 1–3, which deals with the churches. Revelation 6–19 repeatedly uses phrases like 'the Lion of the tribe of Judah' and 'the root of David,' showing a Jewish connection. The 144 evangelists of Revelation 7:1–8; 14:1–5 are all Jewish. The events of the seals, trumpets, and vials will be a partial repetition of the plagues visited upon Egypt and will be for the same purpose, punishing the nations for mistreating Israel. The tribulation will primarily concern Israel and will last through Revelation 6–19, the time when Israel is dealt with. It will be the period known as Daniel's seventieth week. The church age comes between the sixty-ninth and the seventieth week, as is generally understood. The great multitude of Revelation 7:9–17, 15:2–4 and the 144,000 are the only company of redeemed seen on the earth during the whole of Revelation 6–19, but these are not the church but those who come to faith in Christ after the rapture of the church.

The following passage gives conclusive proof that the church will be raptured before the tribulation and before the Antichrist is revealed at the beginning of the week.

> And now you know what is restraining, that he may be revealed in his own time. For the mystery of lawlessness is already at work; only He who now restrains *will do so* until He is taken out of the way. And then the lawless one will be revealed, whom the Lord will consume with the breath of His mouth and destroy with the brightness of His coming.
>
> (2 Thessalonians 2:6–8)

Therefore He says: 'Awake, you who sleep, Arise from the dead, And Christ will give you light.'

See that you walk circumspectly, not as fools but as wise, redeeming the time, because the days are evil. Therefore do not be unwise, but understand what the will of the Lord is.

(Ephesians 5:14–16)

The rapture and the Second Coming of the Lord are practical doctrines that exhort believers to live holy, watchful, and faithful in anticipation of the Lord's coming. It encourages patience, soberness and righteousness, diligence, and purity as well as hope and a life of expectation. This is, certainly, the believer's blessed hope, as Titus declares. Everywhere the Bible discusses the Lord's coming, it is always tied in with a call and admonition to holiness.

For example, 1 John 3:2–3 says:

Beloved, now we are children of God; and it has not yet been revealed what we shall be, but we know that when He is revealed, we shall be like Him, for we shall see Him as He is. And everyone who has this hope in Him purifies Himself, just as he is pure.

QUALIFICATIONS FOR THE RAPTURE

There is only one requirement to qualify for the rapture, and that is one must be 'in Christ' (1 Thessalonians 4:16–17; 2 Corinthians 5:17; 1 Corinthians 15:23). This qualification to be 'in Christ' is expressed differently in scripture:

1. 'Be Christ's' (1 Colossians 5:23, Galatians 5:4)
2. 'Be in Christ' (1 Thessalonians 4:16–17; 2 Corinthians 5:17)
3. 'Be without spot or wrinkle . . . and without blemish' (Ephesians 5:27)

4. 'Have done good' (John 5:28–29)
5. 'Be worthy' (Luke 21:34–36)

This means to go up in the rapture, you must be walking in the light, as He is in the light (1 John 1:7, 2:6, 9–11). It means one must be a new creature in Christ or be 'born again'.

It is true that when believers are taken up in the rapture, some 'professing Christians' will be left behind to go through the tribulation and be martyred. These may not be real Christians and may have just been associated with the church or harbouring some known sin in their lives. This is why it is crucial for every professing Christian to heed the admonitions of scripture and to examine themselves periodically to make sure that they are in right standing with the Lord. And if any potential hindrance is detected, they should correct it immediately with all urgency, because this is a matter of life and death, literally. There are no additional or special qualifications for the rapture apart from 'being in Christ'.

Make sure you meet this criteria so the Lord will count you worthy to escape the horrors of the tribulation.

MAJOR SIGNS OF THE SECOND COMING OF CHRIST

Unlike the rapture, the Lord's Second Coming to the earth to liberate Israel and end the carnage of the tribulation is preceded by a number of prophetic events, which are catalogued by the Bible. These signs and events are too numerous to list here, so a sample of the major events are presented for our readers here.

1. Israel will return to their land. This was fulfilled on 14 May 1948 and *aliya* (a Hebrew word for 'the return of the Jews to the land of Israel') is still ongoing today. 'Now learn this parable from the fig tree: When its branch has already become tender and puts forth leaves, you know that summer is near. So you also, when you see all these things, know that it is near—at the doors!' (Matthew 24:32–33). 'Then He spoke to them a

parable: "Look at the fig tree, and all the trees. When they are already budding, you see and know for yourselves that summer is now near. So you also, when you see these things happening, know that the kingdom of God is near. Assuredly, I say to you, this generation will by no means pass away till all things take place"' (Luke 21:29–32). Israel is celebrating their seventieth anniversary since their return to their ancestral homeland in Canaan. Jesus said the generation that witnessed the rebirth of Israel will not pass away until all these prophesied signs are fulfilled. This means we are pretty close to the Second Coming of the Lord.

2. The love of believers will grow cold. 'And because lawlessness will abound, the love of many will grow cold' (Matthew 24:12). It is apparent we live in a loveless world. The situation is not any better among professing believers. Congregations and ministries are at loggerheads with each other, as are major Christian leaders and pastors. The emergence of cruel child- and sex-trafficking gangs are literally devastating the lives of countless millions. Add to this the new scourge of organ trafficking, where people are literally being killed so their organs will be harvested for sale. It is hard to imagine what has become of the world we live in. The only answer to all these is for the Lord to return soon to take over the earth and save mankind from self-extinction.

3. The incidence of wars, rumours of wars, lawlessness and violence, droughts and famines, earthquakes and natural disasters like volcanoes, tornadoes, hurricanes are increasing.

> And you will hear of wars and rumors of wars. See that you are not troubled; for all these things must come to pass, but the end is not yet. For nation will rise against nation, and kingdom against kingdom. And there will be famines, pestilences, and earthquakes in various places. All these are the beginning of sorrows.
>
> (Matthew 24:6–8)

The incidence of wars going on in the world today is unprecedented. This includes the Arab Spring, the bloody Iraq war, the brutal ongoing war in Syria, the Rwanda genocide, the ravages of Boko Haram in northern Nigeria, the not-too-distant Bosnia genocide, and the terrorist massacres in the UK, France, Belgium, Holland, and the USA.

Add to these the recent devastation of the Caribbean Islands and mainland USA by hurricanes and tornados and the recent floods that devastated USA, UK, France and many other nations are all clear signs of the nearness of the Lord's return. We are barely three months into the year, and there have been over fifty murders in London alone, surpassing the murder rate in New York. It is apparent the political authorities have lost the plot and are not sure how to tackle the menace of knife and gun crimes in London and other major cities in the world.

This painful episode has played on for far too long, devastating young lives needlessly. These days you do not have to be a gang member to get caught up in the murders. My humble take on the situation is that the government should do whatever it can do to fix the traditional family; it should do to enable mums and dads to live together and bring up their children. This can be done through education and support and relevant tax breaks to support families. The policy of prioritising single parenthood, though necessary, is detrimental in the long run to a stable society.

It is not just about the number of police on the streets, even though that has its place; it is about fixing society. And to do that, you should start with the family. And couples need to understand that marriage is not just about them but about the children as well, and so they should find ways to live together in harmony.

4. Heresies, cults, false Christs, and false messiahs will emerge.

'And Jesus answered and said to them: "Take heed that no one deceives you. For many will come in My name, saying, 'I am the Christ,' and will deceive many.

(Matthew 24:4–5)

"Then if anyone says to you, 'Look, here is the Christ!' or 'There!' do not believe it. For false christs and false prophets will rise and show great signs and wonders to deceive, if possible, even the elect. See, I have told you beforehand.

"Therefore if they say to you, 'Look, He is in the desert!' do not go out; or 'Look, He is in the inner rooms!' do not believe it."

(Matthew 23–26)

Cultic groups such as the Fundamentalist Church of the Latter-Day Saints or Mormons, the Church of Christ, the JWs, as well as Christian scientists all claim to be Christian while denying the deity of Christ, His atoning death on the cross, His resurrection and not trusting Him as the only means of man's salvation.

For the time will come when they will not endure sound doctrine, but according to their own desires, because they have itching ears, they will heap up for themselves teachers; and they will turn their ears away from the truth, and be turned aside to fables.

(2 Timothy 4:3–4)

Many Christians today are flocking to prophets and prophetic ministries in a desire to have a quick answer to their problems. Not many value the Word of God in our day, and churches that focus on teaching the Word are generally out of fashion for many Christians. Some of these prophetic ministries are way out there, but because the followers do not know the Word of God for themselves, they continue to patronise these false men and women of God. Put a big red flag against any prophetic word that does not originate in the Word of God. If you can't see it in the Word or at least the spirit of the Word, it does not matter how good the packaging looks. In judging spiritual phenomena, you do not just look at whether something is good or bad. You look at the source. If the source is God and His Word, it does not matter how it may look initially; it is good. The devil manifests as an angel of light, and he often sugar-coats his baits to make them look real good and attractive, but there always is poison within, and the end is pain and death and destruction.

> And this is the condemnation, that the light has
> come into the world, and men loved darkness
> rather than light, because their deeds were evil.
> (John 3:19)

It is not surprising some people would not want anything to do with the church, because they are not prepared to leave their wrong lifestyle behind to embrace the new life of freedom and joy that Christ offers.

> And for this reason God will send them strong
> delusion, that they should believe the lie, that
> they all may be condemned who did not believe
> the truth but had pleasure in unrighteousness.
> (2 Thessalonians 2:11–12)

Alongside the proliferation of cults are their leaders who are claiming to be the Messiah or Christ. Virtually all major continents and most nations have their own false Christs. They include Reverend Jim Jones, Sun Myung Moon, David Koresh, all in the last century. Current false messiahs and false Christs include Sergei Anatolyevitch Torop, otherwise known as the Jesus of Siberia in Russia, and Jose Luis de Jesus Miranda of Puerto Rico, who has lots of Hispanic followers in the United States of America and preaches that so long as you believe in him, it's okay to sin. There is also Lord Maitreya and many others who have drawn large followers after them.

> For such are false apostles, deceitful workers, transforming themselves into apostles of Christ. And no wonder! For Satan himself transforms himself into an angel of light. Therefore it is no great thing if his ministers also transform themselves into ministers of righteousness, whose end will be according to their works.
>
> (2 Corinthians 11:13–15)

> And then the lawless one will be revealed, whom the Lord will consume with the breath of His mouth and destroy with the brightness of His coming. The coming of the lawless one is according to the working of Satan, with all power, signs, and lying wonders, and with all unrighteous deception among those who perish, because they did not receive the love of the truth, that they might be saved.
>
> (2 Thessalonians 2:8–10)

5. Deadly diseases and epidemics (such as birds flu, AIDS, Ebola in West Africa and elsewhere) will emerge. Many of these deadly diseases do not respond to traditional treatments, and some have mutated into deadly strains that have made them virtually untreatable.
6. The gospel will be preached to the ends of the earth:

And this gospel of the kingdom will be preached
in all the world as a witness to all the nations,
and then the end will come.

(Matthew 24:14)

The gospel has been preached in virtually every country on earth. The explosion in satellite and cable TV has ensured that the gospel has penetrated even places where it is literally impossible to preach and evangelise the population, as in many behind the Islamic curtain in the Middle East and elsewhere. There have been marvellous stories of conversions in places like Egypt, Iraq, Iran, Pakistan, and Russia.

As painful as many of these events may be, they point to a future of hope for the world because they indicate that the return of the Lord to right the wrongs of the earth is near. But it all depends on which side you are on. Get on the Lord's side before it is too late.

HIGHLIGHTS ON THE BOOK OF REVELATION

REVELATION CHAPTER 1

This is the revelation that God the Father gave to His Son, Jesus Christ, hence the name the Revelation of Jesus Christ. It is His revelation that God the Father gave to Him. Christ is the central person of the Bible and of this book. As the living Word, the written Word is all about Him, His person, His redemptive work, and what He has said:

> In the volume of the book it is written of Me.
>
> (Hebrews 10:7)

> Search the Scriptures . . . they are they which testify of Me.
>
> (John 5:39)

> He expounded unto them in all the Scriptures the things concerning Himself.
>
> (Luke 27:44)

Not only was the book given to Him and about Him, it is about His final triumph over His enemies, His plan for His children, the church. Christians under pressure have often wondered aloud, 'If Jesus defeated the devil, why did He leave him loose to trouble His children and the people of the world?' Good question. But wait till the end of this book and see how He deals with the devil.

MODE OF TRANSMISSION OF THE REVELATION

God the Father gave the revelation to His Son, Jesus, who in turn gave it to His angel, who also gave it to the apostle John, who gave it to the church.

Revelation 1:1: God the Father–Jesus–the angel–the apostle John–the church.

It is not just revealing anything about the person of Jesus that we did not know already, even though John saw Him in His glory; it is also a revelation of things which must shortly (or quickly) take place, including the events relating to the rapture, the tribulation, and the events leading up to and including the Second Coming of Christ. In all these events, Christ is at the centre. They are all His programme. From Chapter 4 till the end of the book, Chapter 22, it is a series of fast-paced events, covering just seven years in duration. The Second Coming of Christ is the chief theme of the book of Revelation.

Revelation 1:7 declares, 'Behold, He cometh with the clouds and every eye will see Him.'

In Revelation 2:25–26, He declares to His church in Thyatira, 'Hold fast what you have till I come.'

In Revelation 3:3, He warns the church in Sardis, 'Therefore if you will not watch, I will come upon you as a thief.'

Revelation 6:17 declares, 'For the great day of His wrath has come, and who is able to stand.'

In Revelation 22:7, 12, 20, He declares, 'Behold, I am coming quickly.'

In Revelation 22:20, He declares, 'Surely I am coming quickly, Amen.' And the bride and the Spirit reply, 'Even so, come Lord Jesus.'

Then finally, in Revelation 19:11–12, the heavens open for the world to see the Lord Jesus Christ to come the second time as King of Kings and Lord of Lords to take over the kingdoms of this world and rule them for 1,000 years and for all eternity.

Thus, it can be seen that His Second Coming, which will not be a secret event like His first, is the chief theme of the book. Of course, there are many events, players, and characters involved in the book, but they are all facilitating, ancillary to, and leading to His Second Coming.

The angel *signified* the revelation to John. This means this is a book full of signs and symbols to represent the real thing being shown. But these signs and symbols are almost always explained in the context or elsewhere in the book itself or somewhere in the Bible. For the most part, there is no need to go outside the book or the Bible to find the meaning of any symbol or sign.

According to Revelation 1:3, this is the only book in which the believer is promised blessings for reading, hearing, and keeping (observing or doing) the things written in the book. In the same token, there are severe sanctions for tampering with this book.

> For I testify to everyone who hears the words of the prophecy of this book: If anyone adds to these things, God will add to him the plagues that are written in this book; and if anyone takes away from the words of the book of this prophecy, God shall take away his part from the Book of Life, from the holy city, and *from* the things which are written in this book.
>
> (Revelation 22:18–19)

All these underlie the uniqueness of this book and its crucial importance for the believer and the church as the end of the age comes upon us. No wonder it is the most attacked, most maligned, and most mysterious of all the books of the Bible, even more so than the book of Genesis, which has also received a good thrashing as well but has endured the test.

It is a book of judgements, as we can see from the following discussion.

In chapters 2–3, we see Christ pronouncing judgement on His church. God's judgement always begins with His people.

The seven sealed books in chapters 4 and 5 contain the judgements of God that He is about to let loose on the earth and its inhabitants.

There is also the seven trumpet judgements that God unleashes on the earth and its peoples in chapters 8–11. The first trumpet hits the earth with hail, fire, and blood, destroying a third of the vegetation.

The second trumpet hits the sea with a burning mountain, possibly a meteorite, which turns a third of the sea into blood, kills a third of marine life, and destroys a third of ships. The third trumpet is another falling star from heaven, which hits a third of the rivers and the springs of water and turns them bitter. Men died from drinking this bitter water. The fourth trumpet hits the sun, moon, and stars, turning a third of them into darkness so that a third of the day and the night were without light. The fifth trumpet releases a plague of demon locusts from the bottomless pit on the earth with poisonous tails like scorpions, which torment men for five months without killing them. The sixth trumpet releases the four demon angels bound at the great river Euphrates to kill a third of mankind by fire, smoke, and brimstone which come out of their mouths. The seventh trumpet announces that with the sounding of the last trumpet, the mystery of God will be finished. This is about Satan's final doom and incarceration, which was to happen when he is bound and shut up in the bottomless pit following his defeat at the battle of Armageddon (Revelation 20:1).

In chapters 15–16, we see the seven vials (or bowls) of God's wrath upon the earth. The first bowl brings foul and loathsome sores upon the people who have the mark of the beast and those who worship the image of the beast. The second bowl turns the sea into blood and kills every living sea creature. The third bowl turns rivers and springs of waters into blood. The fourth bowl scorches men with great heat from the sun. The fifth bowl plunges the throne of the beast and his kingdom into darkness and men gnaw their tongues because of the pain. The sixth bowl is poured on the great river Euphrates, drying up its waters to open the way for the kings of the east to move their 200,000,000-man army to the battle of Armageddon. It also releases the three unclean spirits like frogs from the mouth of the dragon; from the mouth of the beast and from the mouth of the false prophet, they will to go to the kings of the earth to gather them to the battle of Armageddon. When the seventh bowl is poured into the air, a loud voice issues from heaven to say, 'It is finished.' This is followed by noises, thunder and lightning, and a great and mighty earthquake which will split Jerusalem in three and devastate many cities of the world, literally changing the topography of the entire planet. This is followed by a rain of hail upon men on the earth.

In chapters 17–18, He judges Babylon, the great whore, and politico-economic Babylon respectively. He puts it into the minds of the ten kings of the revised Roman Empire to hate the whore, eat her flesh, and burn her with fire. So religious Babylon is destroyed by the ten kings, but political and economic Babylon, He destroys Himself with fire, never to be inhabited ever again.

The judgement seat of Christ after the rapture may not involve punishment, but judgement. This takes place in heaven after the rapture of the Christians from the earth.

There is also the judgement of the nations into sheep and goat nations (Matthew 25) on His return to earth. This will be based on how nations and individuals treated the Jewish people in the hour of trial during the tribulation. Those who are deemed worthy will enter the millennium kingdom as natural human beings, but those deemed unworthy, or goats, will go straight to hell—alive.

The final judgement is the great white throne judgement, which is the judgement of all those whose names are not found in the Lamb's book of life and cast into the lake of fire and brimstone, which is the final death (Chapter 20).

From this outline, it is apparent there are only two destinies or destinations for man: heaven or hell. This destiny or destination is fixed at the point of death, and whoever you served in your lifetime on earth is whom you will spend all eternity with—the Lord Jesus in heaven or Satan the devil in the lake of fire.

John received the revelation on the Island of Patmos when he was exiled there in AD 79 for his faith.

THE KEY TO UNDERSTANDING THE BOOK

Revelation 1:19 contains the key to a proper understanding of the book. John was asked to 'write the things which you have seen, and the things which are, and the things which will take place after this'.

This gives a threefold division of the book. It is important to keep each division in its place. Also these divisions are consecutive, not concurrent, and any attempt to mix the events of the divisions would lead to confusion. This is the source of much confusion surrounding the book.

1. Part 1: Write *'the things which thou hast seen'*. This is the vision of Christ which John saw before He was asked to write in Revelation 1:13–18.
2. Part 2: Write *'the things which are'*—that is, the things concerning the seven churches in Revelation 2–3. This is the only part of the book that is happening now. None of the things in Revelation 4–22 will be fulfilled until the church age is over and the church is raptured in Revelation 4:2.
3. Part 3: Write *'the things which shall be hereafter'*—that is, after the churches (Revelation 4:1). This means that every single detail in Revelation 4:3 would only be fulfilled after the rapture, when the church is taken away to be with her Lord in heaven.

Part 1: The Things Which Thou Hast Seen—the Vision of the Son of Man (Revelation 1:9–18)

John saw the glorified Christ, and he described eight aspects of His being and presence:

a. His body or appearance: he was clothed with a garment down to the feet and girded about the chest with a golden band.
b. His head and hair were like wool as white as snow.
c. His eyes were like a flame of fire.
d. His feet were like fine brass, as if refined in a furnace.
e. His voice was as the sound of many waters.

f. He had in His right hand seven stars.

g. Out of his mouth went a sharp two-edged sword.

h. And His countenance was like the sun shining in its strength.

When John saw Him, he fell down as dead. 'But he laid His right hand on him and said to him Do not be afraid.' Notice that He did not stop John from worshipping Him but told him not to be afraid. God will always accept worship, but an angel, a holy angel, will always restrain you from worshipping him.

Also notice the aspects of His appearance and being that John noticed; many of these will be in evidence whenever you encounter the true Christ as opposed to an angel or an angel of light. Compare this to the rider on the white horse in Revelation 6:2, and you will know that he cannot be the risen and glorified Christ as all these features of His presence are absent. That must be the Antichrist. You can also know straight away that the rider on the white horse in Revelation 19:11–16 is Christ.

This was a vision John saw momentarily to conclude part 1 of the revelation.

Part 2: The Things Which Are—the Seven Churches (Revelation 2:1, 3:22)

These were seven actual churches in Turkey, whose ruins are still present today. These were selected because they represented the prevailing conditions of churches in John's day. In addition, these will reflect the types of churches that will exist over the entire church age until the rapture of the church. This therefore is a prophetic application of churches in this dispensation.

In addition, there is a lesson in the message to the churches for every individual believer. The Word of God is a mirror that reflects our lives and conditions. As you read it, not only do you see your church somewhere in there, but you see your own individual face or condition somewhere, and you know how Christ addressed that condition or situation and the remedy He prescribed. Heed the admonitions and warnings in there because they are for you and me. For seven times the Lord warns, 'He who has an ear, let him hear what the Spirit says to the churches.' Not only is the Spirit speaking to the corporate church, but as a believer, know that the Spirit is peaking directly to you as an individual with a word of warning or an encouragement.

As we have said before, this is the only part of the entire book that is now being fulfilled. It is after the church age that the events of Revelation 4–22 will begin to be fulfilled.

Part 3: The Things Which Shall Be Hereafter— That Is, after the Church Age

The church age will close with the rapture of the church (Revelation 4:1–2). It is only after the rapture of the church to close the church age that any of the events in Revelation 4–22 will begin to be fulfilled.

So one natural division of the book is as follows:

- Things seen: vision of Christ (Revelation 1)
- Things which are: the seven churches (Revelation 2–3)
- Things hereafter: the rapture of the saints, the scene in heaven, the tribulation, Armageddon, the second advent, millennium or 1,000-year rule, the great white throne judgement, eternity.

The consecutive nature of the books, expressed by the words 'after this' or 'after these things', is repeated all through the book in Revelation 1:19; 4:1; 7:1, 9; 15:5; 18:1; 19:1 to underline the fact that the sequence of events runs all through the book from beginning to finish.

Also, another feature of the book we mentioned earlier was the fact that it uses a lot of signs and symbols to represent what is being conveyed and that these symbols and signs are always explained in the context or somewhere in the book itself.

For instance, we learnt at the beginning, in Chapter 1:1, that Jesus gave the revelation to His angel to reveal it to John. In Revelation 22:16, the Lord Jesus declared, 'I, Jesus, have sent my angel to testify to you these things in the churches.' But when John attempted to worship this same angel earlier on, in Revelation 22:8–9, the angel protested, saying he was a fellow servant and a fellow prophet like John.

> I, John, am the one who heard and saw these things. And when I had heard and seen them, I fell down to worship at the feet of the angel who had been showing them to me. But he said to me, 'Don't do that! I am a fellow servant with you and with your fellow prophets and with all who keep the words of this scroll. Worship God!'

This was also alluded to in Revelation 19:10. So the angel was actually a man. Based on this revelation, we can conclude that all the angels to which the seven letters to the churches were addressed are the human pastors or leaders of those churches. An angel is simply a servant or a messenger, and Jesus said that He holds these in His right hand. But Hebrews 2:16 says, 'He does not give aid to angels but He gives aid to the seed of Abraham.' Jesus would not hold any spirit angel in His hand, but He does His human angels. In fact, in Psalm 91:12, He says he gives His angels charge over His servants and cause His angels to bear them up in their hands.

By the same token, we are able to conclude that the great sign of the sun-clothed woman in Revelation 12:1–6 is national Israel, who gives birth to the male child who are the 144,000 Jewish evangelists from the 12 tribes of Israel in Revelation 7 to evangelise the world in the absence of the church on earth. We know this by the account of Joseph's dream in Genesis 37:9–10.

In line with the predominant use of symbols, there are several depictions of angels in the book, some of which are likely to be the Lord Jesus Christ Himself appearing as an angel messenger, judging by His appearance in the vision John had seen earlier of the exalted Christ.

He seems to be the angel who seals the 144,000 Jewish evangelists in Revelation 7:2 and also the priestly angel with the golden censer who offers the prayers of the saints on the golden altar to God as the only mediator between God and man in Revelation 8:1–3.

He is the angel redeemer clothed with a cloud, His face shinning as the sun, with a rainbow around His head, and whose voice is as the voice of a lion, referring to the two witnesses as 'My two witnesses' in Revelation 10:5, 8–10; 11:1.

He is the messenger angel who lights up the earth with His glory. Angels may have some glory, but none to light up the whole earth as seen in Revelation 18:1.

He may also be the angel who binds Satan and casts him into the bottomless pit and shuts him up for 1,000 years. He is the only 'stronger man' who can bind the 'strong man' and spoil his goods as in Revelation 20:1–3.

The rapture of the church takes place in Revelation 4:1–2, where John sees an open door in heaven and commanded by a trumpet-like voice to 'Come up here' to be shown things which must take place after this—that is, the churches. Could this be the same shout of the Lord in 1 Thessalonians 4:16 to summon believers to come up in the rapture?

Immediately after the summon, John is in heaven, around the very throne room itself. Here John sees twenty-four elders around the throne, worshipping God. Of these, twelve are the New Testament apostles of the Lamb and twelve are the Old Testament patriarchs who were the heads of the twelve tribes of Israel (Matthew 19:28; Luke 22:29). There is evidence that the Old Testament saints and the New Testament saints are all raptured together. So John and these twenty-four elders are representative of this first company of raptured saints. Not only that, but when this group of saints sing their song of praise before God, as every group does, in Revelation 5:9–19, they declare that they have been redeemed from every tribe and tongue and people and nation, which means the multitudes in heaven go beyond the twenty-four elders, who all happen to be Jewish.

> And they sang a new song, saying:
> 'You are worthy to take the scroll,
> And to open its seals;
> For You were slain,
> And have redeemed us to God by Your blood

Out of every tribe and tongue and people and nation,
And have made us kings and priests to our God;
And we shall reign on the earth.'
(Revelation 5:9–10)

In heaven, John saw the Father, sitting on the throne, with the twenty-four white-robed elders sitting, wearing crowns of gold. He saw the four living creatures, each with six wings and full of eyes. This account clearly shows that heaven is a real place, a planet out there, with streets and thrones and inhabitants like we have on earth. The earth was patterned after heaven, even though it is a poor copy, made worse by the blight of sin and the curse.

In Chapter 5, Jesus is the only one qualified or worthy to take the scroll from the right hand of the one seated on the throne because He is the one that redeemed mankind, as Revelation 5:9 declares. This sealed scroll contains the judgements coming upon the world during the seven-year tribulation that is about to break loose.

In Revelation 6:1, when the Lamb (Jesus, the Lamb of God, who takes away the sin of the world (John 1:29)) opens the first seal, one of the four living creatures says with a voice like thunder, 'Come.' It was only there and then that the rider on the white horse, the Antichrist, makes his debut on the world stage. The Antichrist cannot come on his own accord. He has to be let in by the express invitation of Christ, and this would only be after the rapture of the church. Notice that he has a bow but no arrow and a crown was given him, and he goes out conquering and to conquer.

The opening of the second seal ushers in the rider on the fiery red horse, representing war, followed by famine and death. This is what the Antichrist will usher in: wars, famine, and death. Revelation 6:8 says this mass death will come through the wars and hunger or famine by the spirit of death and by wild beasts of the earth, which might well include demonic spirits. In fact, his first act of war would be to overthrow three of the ten leaders of the revised Roman Empire (Daniel 7:8, 24).

REVELATION 7: THE 144,000 JEWISH EVANGELISTS

These are selected from all the tribes of Israel except the tribe of Dan, and we can safely assume that this is because none of the tribe of Dan is saved at this time. Remember that the 7-year tribulation is God's final period in dealing with Israel out of the 490 years He set aside for Israel (Daniel 9:24). He had to suspend His dealings with Israel after they rejected their Messiah and crucified Him at the end of the 69th week, or after 483 years.

According to Luke 19:28–44:

The Triumphal Entry

When He had said this, He went on ahead, going up to Jerusalem. And it came to pass, when He drew near to Bethphage and Bethany, at the mountain called Olivet, *that* He sent two of His disciples, saying, 'Go into the village opposite *you*, where as you enter you will find a colt tied, on which no one has ever sat. Loose it and bring *it here*. And if anyone asks you, "Why are you loosing *it?*" thus you shall say to him, 'Because the Lord has need of it.'"

So those who were sent went their way and found *it* just as He had said to them. But as they were loosing the colt, the owners of it said to them, 'Why are you loosing the colt?'

And they said, 'The Lord has need of him.' Then they brought him to Jesus. And they threw their own clothes on the colt, and they set Jesus on him. And as He went, *many* spread their clothes on the road.

Then, as He was now drawing near the descent of the Mount of Olives, the whole multitude of the disciples began to rejoice and praise God with a loud voice for all the mighty works they had seen, saying:

'Blessed *is* the King who comes in the name of the LORD!

Peace in heaven and glory in the highest!'

And some of the Pharisees called to Him from the crowd, 'Teacher, rebuke Your disciples.'

But He answered and said to them, 'I tell you that if these should keep silent, the stones would immediately cry out.'

Now as He drew near, He saw the city and wept over it, saying, 'If you had known, even you, especially in this your day, the things *that make* for your peace! But now they are hidden from your eyes. For days will come upon you when your enemies will build an embankment around you, surround you and close you in on every side, and level you, and your children within you, to the ground; and they will not leave in you one stone upon another, because you did not know the time of your visitation.'

In less that forty years after the Jews rejected their Messiah, precisely in AD 70, the Roman army besieged Jerusalem and destroyed the city and their temple, killing over one million of them in the process. Life for the Jews and Israel has never been the same since.

So after the Jews rejected their long-awaited Messiah-King on the first Palm Sunday, on 6 April AD 32, and proceeded to crucify Him five days later, God suspended His plan for Israel and the fulfilment of His promises made to their fathers and their promised kingdom. That suspension has been going on for almost two thousand years now. After setting Israel aside, He turned His attention to the Gentiles to establish the church and take a people from among them to rule and reign with Him in the millennium and for all eternity.

So He has reserved the last 7 years of this age what is left of the 490 years reserved for Israel and Jerusalem to finish His dealings with Israel and bring them into the bond of the new covenant and fulfil His promises to their fathers, hence His using Jewish evangelists to evangelise the world in the absence of the church on earth. The first thing God does is to send His angel to seal each of these 144,000 with His seal of protection for their dangerous assignment of evangelising the world in those dangerous times (Revelation 7:3). These are born by the nation of Israel. Revelation 12:1–5 states:

> Now a great sign appeared in heaven: a woman clothed with the sun, with the moon under her feet, and on her head, a garland of twelve stars. Then being with child, she cried out in labour and in pain to give birth. And another sign appeared in heaven: behold a great fiery-red dragon having seven heads and ten horns and seven diadems on his heads. His tail drew a third of the stars of heaven and threw them to the earth. And the dragon stood before the woman who was ready to give birth, to devour her Child as soon as it was born. She bore a male Child who was to rule all nations with a rod of iron. And her Child was caught up to God and His throne.

Compare this with Joseph's dream in Genesis 37:9–10, and see the uncanny similarities in the two accounts.

> Then he dreamed still another dream and told it to his brothers, and said, 'Look, I have dreamed another dream. And this time, the sun, the moon, and the eleven stars bowed down to me.'

So he told *it* to his father and his brothers; and his father rebuked him and said to him, 'What *is* this dream that you have dreamed? Shall your mother and I and your brothers indeed come to bow down to the earth before you?'

The Revelation 12 account is not the birth of Christ but of these Jewish evangelists. Remember that the book is consecutive and everything from Chapter 4 till the end is in the future, so it cannot be the birth of Jesus Christ, which had taken place a couple of thousands of years before this episode (which is still future) happens. After they finish their assigned work of evangelising the inhabitants of the world, they are raptured together as a company in the middle of the week (Revelation 12:5); that is the end of the first three and a half years just when the Antichrist comes on the scene and seeks to destroy them. They are then seen in heaven (Revelation 14:1–5). Like every company of raptured saints, they sing a song of praise unto the living God (Revelation 14:3), but we are not told the words of their song, except that no one could learn their song. This is because their song will reflect their unique redemption experience, which will not make sense to any other company of believers who have gone through their unique experience. We are told that they will follow the Lamb wherever He goes, ruling and reigning with Him for all eternity. We are told that these were virgins who have not defiled themselves with women. By this time, the world would have been so polluted and defiled with the whore demonic religion, but these people would not have been tainted by this idolatrous world religion, which many of their Jewish compatriots would have come to embrace. So they are virgins in a spiritual sense, not having defiled themselves with idolatrous worship. This company of saints would be responsible for many of the multitudes of people who would come to faith in the first half of the tribulation. They are raptured just in time to avert the appearance of the Antichrist on the world scene. Their main opposition will come from the whore religious system and the ten nations of the revised Roman Empire.

After these are raptured, God will bring His two witnesses who have been standing before His throne for several thousands of years, Elijah and Enoch, to come and be witnesses to the Jews, but these will be based only in Jerusalem, unlike the 144,000, who will go all over the world wherever God needs them.

> 'Two olive trees *are* by it, one at the right of the bowl and the other at its left.' So I answered and spoke to the angel who talked with me, saying, 'What *are* these, my lord?'
>
> Two olive trees are by it, one at the right of the bowl and the other at its left
>
> Then the angel who talked with me answered and said to me, 'Do you not know what these are?'
>
> Then I answered and said to him, 'What *are* these two olive trees—at the right of the lampstand and at its left?' And I further answered and said to him, 'What *are these* two olive branches that *drip* into the receptacles of the two gold pipes from which the golden *oil* drains?'
>
> Then he answered me and said, 'Do you not know what these are?'
>
> And I said, 'No, my lord.'
>
> So he said, 'These are the two anointed ones, who stand beside the Lord of the whole earth.'
> (Zechariah 4:3–5, 11–14)

These two prophets will prophesy in Jerusalem for three and a half years, and they will be a source of torment to the Antichrist and his people, but God will supernaturally protect them so they cannot be harmed. They will be given power to shut the heavens so that it does not rain for three and a half years. They have power to turn waters to blood and to strike the earth with all kinds of plagues at will.

When they finish their prophecy, God will remove His protection over them and allow them to be killed by that demonic prince known as the beast that ascends out of the bottomless pit, or the prince of Grecia. The text says that when they are killed, the Antichrist will not allow them to be buried. Their dead bodies will lie in the street for three and a half days in Jerusalem. At the end of the three and a half days, the breath of God will enter them, and they will stand on their feet. Then the voice of God will resound: 'Come up here.' And they will ascend and be raptured to heaven in a cloud in the full glare of the world's media.

Now, what would the people of the world say to this open rapture this time? The earlier mass rapture of believers may have taken the world by surprise, being generally a secret event, but this one would be captured by the world's media, all major TV and cable networks, the Internet, and all major satellite media. This is God's open challenge to the people of the world—to put their trust in Him and not to believe the lies they are being fed.

There are several arguments to prove the identity of these two prophets, but the fact that they are killed at the end of their testimony proves conclusively that they are Elijah and Enoch, the only two people that lived and never tasted death and who must of necessity come to taste their quota of death. According to Hebrews 9:27: 'It is appointed for men to die once, and after this, the judgement.' If it were someone like Moses and some other prophet, these could not die a second time and certainly could not be killed by the demonic beast. The text also says that God will give them power to fulfil their ministry, so this is not about power they exercised previously in their earlier ministry even though the dynamics could be similar (Revelation 11:1–14).

This is about Revelation 12:7–17. The first six verses of Revelation 12 deals with the birth of the 144,000 Jewish evangelists, which we have covered elsewhere in this book. But verses 7 to the end of the chapter is about an epic cosmic battle between God and His angelic forces and Satan and his demonic hordes. Man has for centuries been asking God to leave him alone to run things. Alas, he is about to have his wish come true. During this time, about the middle of the tribulation, God and His angelic army will actually evict Satan and his demons from the second heavens, where they are currently headquartered, and throw them down unto the earth. During this time, Satan and his demons would actually be living on planet earth. That is why the text says, 'Woe to the inhabitants of the earth and the sea! For the devil has come down to you, having great wrath, because he knows he has a short time.' He and his demons will head straight to Babylon.

According to Revelation 18:1–2:

> After this I saw another angel coming down from heaven. He had great authority, and the earth was illuminated by his splendor. With a mighty voice he shouted:
> 'Fallen! Fallen is Babylon the Great!
> She has become a dwelling for demons
> and a haunt for every impure spirit,
> a haunt for every unclean bird,
> a haunt for every unclean and detestable animal.'

This is because Babylon, the place of man's first rebellion against God, is the place Satan has chosen to be his seat of government to operate from and from where to plan all his murderous activities in his final efforts to exterminate the Jews and the tribulation saints of the closing hours of this age. It will be the place of man's last and final rebellion against God.

> Then the angel who talked with me came out and said to me, 'Lift your eyes now, and see what this is that goes forth.'

> So I asked, 'What is it?' And he said, 'It is a basket that is going forth.'

He also said, 'This is their resemblance throughout the earth: Here is a lead disc lifted up, and this is a woman sitting inside the basket' then he said, 'This is Wickedness!' And he thrust her down into the basket, and threw the lead cover over its mouth. Then I raised my eyes and looked, and there were two women, coming with the wind in their wings; for they had wings like the wings of a stork, and they lifted up the basket between earth and heaven.

So I said to the angel who talked with me, 'Where are they carrying the basket?'

And he said to me, 'To build a house for it in the land of Shinar; when it is ready, the basket will be set there on its base.'

(Zechariah 5:5–11)

The construction of this site is what Zechariah saw in a vision in Chapter 5:5–11 to build a house for the woman in the disk called Wickedness in the land of Shinar. Yes, Babylon was the site of the first rebellion by man against God, and it will be the last. The city will be rebuilt and will come into great prominence politically and economically and, in the end of days, spiritually as well. That is why God will overthrow her with fire, never to be inhabited ever again. It will be the headquarters of the whore religious system, which was the woman Zachariah saw and also John saw in Revelation 17.

In Revelation 17, we are told that this false religious system will exercise great influence over many national leaders, peoples, multitudes, nations, and tongues. God Himself with cause the ten nations of the Antichrist to give their power to this religious system, but when the Antichrist rises to power in the middle of the week, after gaining control over all the ten nations of revised Rome, he, with the ten nations, will turn against the whore and destroy her. The Antichrist will destroy the false religious system because he wants to be the only object of worship by all the peoples of the world. That is why shortly after this, he puts his image in the holy of holies in the temple in Jerusalem and demand the Jews worship him as God. This is what causes the Jews to rebel against him, drawing his murderous wrath against them, and he will seek to exterminate them completely. The whore and the ten nations of revised Rome will be the main source of persecution against the believers and the Jews in the first half of the tribulation.

> I saw the woman, drunk with the blood of the saints
> and with the blood of the martyrs of Jesus. And when I
> saw her, I marveled with great amazement.
>
> (Revelation 17:6)

Babylon is overthrown when God puts it in the minds of the ten nations to turn against the harlot and destroy her because of her murder of God's people.

Then finally in Revelation 18, God destroys the literal, political, economic Babylon with fire for the depravity of its inhabitants and how they have corrupted the whole world. This, unlike religious Babylon, is a literal, physical destruction with fire and extreme violence. She becomes the Antichrist's political and economic headquarters from the beginning of the second half of the tribulation, though he will later operate from Jerusalem. We are told of the influence of Babylon over the kings of the world, the sailors, and the merchants of the world and how she will make many wealthy by the abundance of her wealth and commerce. So naturally when she is destroyed by God with fire, we see the kings of the earth who committed fornication and lived luxuriously with her weep and lament for her when they see the smoke of her burning. So do the merchants of the earth who became rich by her. This will be the case for every shipmaster, all who travel by ship, and sailors. And the many that trade on the sea will all cry out when they see the smoke of her burning.

In Revelation 6:9–10, *the lesser tribulation saints cry to God to avenge their murders.*

When He opened the fifth seal, I saw under the altar
the souls of those who had been slain for the word of
God and for the testimony which they held. And they
cried with a loud voice, saying, 'How long, O Lord, holy
and true, until You judge and avenge our blood on those
who dwell on the earth?'

We see God answering their prayers and avenging their murders,
as these were all planned and perpetrated from, guess where, Babylon.

'Rejoice over her, O heaven, and you holy apostles and
prophets, for God has avenged you on her!'

For true and righteous are His judgments, because He
has judged the great harlot who corrupted the earth
with her fornication; and He has avenged on her the
blood of His servants shed by her.'
(Revelation 18:20, 19:2)

Why was God so incensed with Babylon? Let us look at Babylon's long
history and idolatrous career. Babylon was the cradle of civilization, the
birthplace of mankind. It was man's ancestral home and place of origin.

And Babylon, the glory of kingdoms,
The beauty of the Chaldeans' pride,
Will be as when God overthrew Sodom and Gomorrah.
(Isaiah 13:19)

'And look, here comes a chariot of men with a pair of
horsemen!'
Then he answered and said,
'Babylon is fallen, is fallen!
And all the carved images of her gods
He has broken to the ground.'
(Isaiah 21:9)

But wild beasts of the desert will lie there,
And their houses will be full of owls;
Ostriches will dwell there,
And wild goats will caper there.

(Isaiah 13:21)

For it is the day of the LORD's vengeance,
The year of recompense for the cause of Zion.
Its streams shall be turned into pitch,
And its dust into brimstone;
Its land shall become burning pitch.
It shall not be quenched night or day;
Its smoke shall ascend forever.
From generation to generation it shall lie waste;
No one shall pass through it forever and ever.
But the pelican and the porcupine shall possess it,
Also the owl and the raven shall dwell in it.
And He shall stretch out over it
The line of confusion and the stones of emptiness.
They shall call its nobles to the kingdom,
But none shall be there, and all its princes shall be nothing.
And thorns shall come up in its palaces,
Nettles and brambles in its fortresses;
It shall be a habitation of jackals,
A courtyard for ostriches.
The wild beasts of the desert shall also meet with the jackals,
And the wild goat shall bleat to its companion;
Also the night creature shall rest there,
And find for herself a place of rest.

(Isaiah 34:8–14)

Sit in silence, and go into darkness,
O daughter of the Chaldeans;

For you shall no longer be called
The Lady of Kingdoms.
I was angry with My people;
I have profaned My inheritance,
And given them into your hand.
You showed them no mercy;
On the elderly you laid your yoke very heavily.
And you said, 'I shall be a lady forever,'
So that you did not take these things to heart,
Nor remember the latter end of them.

(Isaiah 47:5–11)

Babylon has also been a great persecutor of the covenant people of God, the Jewish people throughout their history, and even those in modern times, from Nebuchadnezzar to Saddam Husain. President Saddam Husain was a major contributor to the Martyr Fund for Palestinians, which rewarded Palestinians who murdered Jews and their families. Such actions do not escape God's attention, and He is sure to visit with retributive judgement sooner rather than later.

'Therefore hear this now, you who are given to pleasures,
Who dwell securely,
Who say in your heart, "I am, and there is no one else besides me;
I shall not sit as a widow,
Nor shall I know the loss of children";
But these two things shall come to you
In a moment, in one day:
The loss of children, and widowhood.
They shall come upon you in their fullness
Because of the multitude of your sorceries,
For the great abundance of your enchantments.
'For you have trusted in your wickedness;
You have said, "No one sees me";
Your wisdom and your knowledge have warped you;

And you have said in your heart,
"I am, and there is no one else besides me."
Therefore evil shall come upon you;
You shall not know from where it arises.
And trouble shall fall upon you;
You will not be able to put it off.
And desolation shall come upon you suddenly,
Which you shall not know.

(Isaiah 47:8–11)

As a final monument to her rebellious career and her corruption of the world, God will open a hole in the site of Babylon from where people can see into the fires of hell and the torment of souls happening in the lake of fire. This will be God's final warning to all mankind that rebellion does not pay in the end.

And they shall go forth and look
Upon the corpses of the men
Who have transgressed against Me.
For their worm does not die,
And their fire is not quenched.
They shall be an abhorrence to all flesh.

(Isaiah 66:24)

This author firmly believes that the first Iraq war of 2003 between America and her allies and Iraq was God's judgement on Iraq, which the prophet Jeremiah wrote extensively about in Jeremiah 50 and 51. In it, the prophet declares 'Because you have contended against the Lord' in Jeremiah 50:24. The verse 25 declares, 'The Lord has opened His armoury, And has brought out the weapons of His indignation; For this is the work of the Lord God of hosts in the land of the Chaldeans.' Hear how God records the world's reaction to the fall of Baghdad, the day Saddam's statue fell, on Saturday, 15 February 2003: 'At the noise of the taking of Babylon The earth trembles and the cry is heard among the nations.' On that day, there were worldwide protests and demonstrations in all the major capitals against the invasion. There is coming yet another judgement on Babylon, and this time God is going to destroy her with fire, never to be inhabited again. This is all in judgement for her rebellion and destruction of God's heritage, the Jewish people.

Revelation 19 is an account of heaven's celebration over the judgement and fall of Babylon, not forgetting that many of the inhabitants of heaven have been martyred by Babylon and therefore have every cause to rejoice over her judgement and eventual destruction.

The rest of the chapter takes in the marriage supper of the Lamb, which will be the last act of the raptured saints in heaven just before their return back to the earth to liberate the Jews and destroy the Antichrist and his forces at the battle of Armageddon and begin the millennial reign of Christ on the earth.

> Then I heard the man clothed in linen, who was above the waters of the river, when he held up his right hand and his left hand to heaven, and swore by Him who lives forever, that it shall be for a time, times, and half a time; and when the power of the holy people has been completely shattered, all these things shall be finished.
>
> (Daniel 12:7)

This means the one event that prompts the Lord's urgent return to the earth is when the power of the holy people is completely shattered—when Israel is finally defeated by the Antichrist and his forces and they will be in no position to defend themselves any more and, for the first time, will be in real danger of total extermination. This is what it will take for them to cry out to the God of their fathers and what it will take for Jesus to come down to their rescue and restoration.

> And it shall come to pass in all the land,'
> Says the LORD,
> '*That* two-thirds in it shall be cut off *and* die,
> But *one*–third shall be left in it:
> I will bring the *one*–third through the fire,

127

Will refine them as silver is refined,
And test them as gold is tested.
They will call on My name,
And I will answer them.
I will say, "This *is* My people"
And each one will say, "The LORD *is* my God.""

(Zechariah 13:8–9)

Two-thirds of the Jewish people will be cut off, but one-third will be left in it to go into the millennium to inherit their promised national restoration and blessing. I believe the surviving third that are saved with be the remnant who accepts and puts their trust in Jesus as Lord and saviour. God will use that to purge the land of all rebels and idolatry for good.

Lest we forget, all the martyred tribulation saints, both those of the minor tribulation and the great tribulation, are raptured together just in time at the end of the tribulation to partake of the marriage supper of the Lamb (Revelation 15:2–4).

At Armageddon, the Antichrist will be destroyed by the Lord Jesus, but the false prophet and the beast, the demonic prince of Grecia, will be cast alive into the lake of fire. The rest of the army of the Antichrist will be destroyed by Christ. All the birds of the air and the beasts of the field who have been invited to the great supper of the Lord will feast on the flesh of the fallen soldiers and their horses. It will be a place of such carnage as the world has never seen before. This is graphically described in Revelation 14:17–20:

> Then another angel came out of the temple which is in heaven, he also having a sharp sickle.
>
> And another angel came out from the altar, who had power over fire, and he cried with a loud cry to him who had the sharp sickle, saying, 'Thrust in your sharp sickle and gather the clusters of the vine of the earth, for her grapes are fully ripe.' So the angel thrust his sickle into

the earth and gathered the vine of the earth, and threw *it* into the great winepress of the wrath of God. And the winepress was trampled outside the city, and blood came out of the winepress, up to the horses' bridles, for one thousand six hundred furlongs.

But the Antichrist will be killed, as the following scriptures attests:

And then the lawless one will be revealed, whom the Lord will consume with the breath of His mouth and destroy with the brightness of His coming.

(2 Thessalonians 2:8)

I watched then because of the sound of the pompous words which the horn was speaking; I watched till the beast was slain, and its body destroyed and given to the burning flame.

(Daniel 7:11)

He shall strike the earth with the rod of His mouth,

And with the breath of His lips He shall slay the wicked.

(Isaiah 11:4b)

All these are proof that the Antichrist is a mortal man, whom Christ will destroy at Armageddon.

Chapter 20 opens with the capture and binding of Satan with a great chain by a mighty angel at Armageddon and his incarceration in the bottomless pit. The angel shuts him up and sets a seal on him for a thousand years. This binding angel may well be the Lord Jesus Christ Himself, as explained in the opening chapter. After the thousand years is over, Satan will be released from his prison in the bottomless pit, and he will come and deceive those who were born during the millennium, who have never known the deceptions of Satan. Many will follow him, and they will besiege Jerusalem and try to destroy it, but fire will come out of heaven from God and devour them. Then the devil will be captured and put in the lake of fire, where the beast and the false prophet are (still alive after a thousand years). Finally, God is putting the devil in his right place so all mankind will know that Satan and God had never been in the same league and never will.

It is after the incarceration of Satan in the lake of fire that the unrighteous dead will be summoned to the great white throne judgement before God the Father in heaven. They are all guilty and already condemned, but God is going to tell them individually why they have been sentenced to the lake of fire. Currently, they are in hell, awaiting the final trial and then judgement, and then to the lake of fire, where they will spend eternity in indescribable torment and agony. Judgement here is for all ungodly humans whose names are not in the book of life and for all satanic spirits who, with Satan, rebelled against God. Right now many of these rebellious angels are in various holding centres, awaiting final judgement, as described in the following scriptures:

> And the angels who did not keep their proper domain, but left their own abode, He has reserved in everlasting chains under darkness for the judgment of the great day.
>
> (Jude 6)

> For if God did not spare the angels who sinned, but cast them down to hell and delivered them into chains of darkness, to be reserved for judgment.
>
> (2 Peter 2:4)

When the great white throne judgement is over, then the God will renovate the earth and make it as new, removing everything that comes into the world as a result of the fall of man and the resulting curse.

> But the day of the Lord will come as a thief in the night, in which the heavens will pass away with a great noise, and the elements will melt with fervent heat; both the earth and the works that are in it will be burned up.
>
> (2 Peter 3:10)

> But the heavens and the earth, *which* are now preserved by the same word, are reserved for fire until the day of judgment and perdition of ungodly men.
>
> (2 Peter 3:7)

Some of these spirits are free to roam the earth and the heavens, and it is these who are the foot soldiers of Satan and working hard for him to deceive mankind with the ultimate agenda to take them to hell with them. He only comes to steal, to kill, and to destroy, and the lake of fire is the ultimate destruction the devil can visit on any human.

Then the New Jerusalem, where the saints would dwell, will come from heaven into the earth's atmosphere. Then God will move His throne from heaven to come and be with His children on earth in the New Jerusalem, where we will live with Him forever and ever, ruling and reigning over the natural but immortal people, who would be living in the New Earth. In the New Jerusalem, there will be no need of the sun or of the moon because of the brilliance of the Lord's glory, which would illuminate it. The sun's light will be like shinning a torchlight at midday. Its light would hardly be noticeable. We can and will eat and drink, but we don't need to do so to sustain our lives as we now do on earth. Everyone, no matter their age, will look healthy and youthful, with no missing body parts such as eyes, limbs, teeth, or hair. What a glorious future the Father has planned for His children!

Yes, the natural but immortal people from the New Earth would be free to visit the New Jerusalem as and when they choose.

The best part of it all is that we shall see the face of the Father.

And he showed me a pure river of water of life, clear as crystal, proceeding from the throne of God and of the Lamb. In the middle of its street, and on either side of the river, *was* the tree of life, which bore twelve fruits, each *tree* yielding its fruit every month. The leaves of the tree *were* for the healing of the nations. And there shall be no more curse, but the throne of God and of the Lamb shall be in it, and His servants shall serve Him. They shall see His face, and His name *shall be* on their foreheads. There shall be no night there: They need no lamp nor light of the sun, for the Lord God gives them light. And they shall reign forever and ever.

(Revelation 22:1–5)

The time for the fulfilment of these great mysteries is near indeed. That is why every person needs to consider where they are going to spend eternity. The moment you die, your eternal state is fixed, and you cannot change your mind. It may be too late. These may seem to you as fairly tales, but they are the true Word of God. God has sent His Word to you because He loves you so much and wants to spend eternity with you in heaven. Do not reject His generous offer of salvation because if you do, you will regret it for all eternity, but it will be too late. The book of Revelation provides an exciting panorama of soon-coming events. While some things in the book, such as the coming tribulation, the wicked person the Bible calls the Antichrist and his mark of the beast, may appear scary and frightening, you have nothing to fear from any of these when you put your trust in Christ as your Lord and Saviour to protect you. You will not witness any of those terrible things coming to the world. Even if you should go through them, as some people believe, which this author does not share, He is still able to protect you. The only way you keep your life is to give it to Christ by inviting Him to take residence in you by His Holy Spirit. Today if you will hear His voice, do not harden your heart.

THE COMING WORLDWIDE MASSACRE OF TRIBULATION SAINTS

The church of God is soon to be raptured from the earth to heaven. The doctrine of imminence means this can take place at any time without warning or precondition. 'But our salvation is closer than when we first believed.' In the wake of the rapture, countless millions, possibly billions, of people will come to faith in the Lord Jesus and be saved. Finally, they will wake up to the rude fact that their friends and families who were 'fanatical' about Jesus were right. Thus, the morning following the rapture will see most churches packed to capacity with those who were associated with the church but were not ready to go in the rapture as well as multitudes who finally wakened to the fact that Christianity must be true after all. These are known as the tribulation saints. They are not part of the church but are saved after the rapture of the church. Countless millions of others will literally go insane when they realise they've been left behind.

Matthew 24–25 is Jesus' response to a question by His disciples about the signs of His Second Coming. In Matthew 24:3, they asked Him, 'Tell us, when will these things be? And what will be the sign of your coming, and of the end of the age?' The Lord tells three parables—first about the conditions that preceded Noah's flood, then the landlord whose house was broken into by thieves, and the wise and foolish virgins. And all three situations are ended with an exhortation to 'Watch, watch, watch' (Matthew 24:42, 44 and 25:13). It is clear in Matthew 25, that the five wise virgins have made personal decisions for Christ and were born-again (possibly Spirit-filled) believers, but more importantly, they were ready for their Lord. The five foolish virgins, well, they were closely associated with the church in several respects, but for whatever reason, they were not watchful or ready or prepared for the Lord's return. Sadly, our churches today are full of Christians who are simply not ready.

'Behold, the Bridegroom comes, go ye out to meet Him'—this certainly is alluding to the rapture because at the rapture, the bride goes out to meet the Bridegroom in the air. He does not come down to us on the earth. Also note that after meeting the groom, they go straight to the wedding feast, which alludes to the marriage supper of the Lamb, which follows the rapture in heaven (Revelation 19:9).

The five foolish virgins who came knocking after the Bridegroom's departure are those people who will perhaps realise their mistake and will decide to commit to the Lord and get born-again *after* the rapture. We know these people very well because we've all got them in our families and circle of friends. Perhaps they have often argued with us about so-called 'contentious' aspects of the gospel. They often argue that faith is all about your heart, and rightly so, but the only problem is that faith in the heart must be worked out to become faith in your outward life, visible through our daily actions and lifestyle. There is nothing like a secret Christian. You are either in or you are out.

These people may be regular church attenders but have never made a decision for Christ, or they are living a lie or with a known sin and assuming it does not matter. They could have been taught rather wrongly that they have to earn their salvation by doing a set number of good works. They may have come to believe that walking in the anointing and performing signs and wonders meant God approves of them. They may believe wrongly that because they are 'good people' who don't do certain sinful stuff, there is no way God could say no to them, or they put their trust in their church or denomination. Some may actually know the way of salvation, but hey, they want to wait and do it later. Give them time to enjoy themselves just a little bit before they really commit. These understand their need for salvation, but their common refrain is 'I'm not ready yet'. Somehow, all these people have assumed that familiarity with the Lord, knowing 'about' Him and His ministry, giving to the cause of Christ, or supporting Christian or church programmes are sufficient substitutes for salvation, as is clearly illustrated by the Lord Jesus in Matthew 7:23, 25:12 and Luke 13:25. Some may simply have been in the wrong churches where a different gospel was preached. Of these, there are many. But the testimony of scripture is clear on this: 'Unless one is born again, he cannot see the kingdom of God' (John 3:3). 'And this is eternal life, that they may know You, the only true God, and Jesus Christ whom You have sent.'

When these peoples wake up one day and realise that the Christian fanatics have all disappeared in the rapture, they will go on their knees in prayer to commit their lives to Christ, but alas, it would be too late, as many of them would be martyred for their faith. People believe wrongly that the Lord will protect these tribulation believers so nothing will happen to them. It is always important to let the scriptures speak for itself and not to insert our own pet ideas and notions. In the tribulation, God's attitude towards all the inhabitants of the earth is completely different from what it is under the current period of grace. Listen to what the Bible says in Revelation 13:7, 17:17 about the Antichrist: 'It was granted to him to make war with the saints and to overcome them. And authority was given him over every tribe, tongue and nation.' This is reiterated in Daniel 7:21: 'I was watching and the same horn was making war with the saints, and prevailing against them.' In Revelation 6:9–11 when the first batch of tribulation martyrs cry out to God for vengeance against their murderers, God's answer to them was 'Wait till the number of those who would be killed as you were is complete and we do not hear of them again'. This is until Revelation 18:20, 24, when the massacre is complete.

In the absence of the raptured church, God will raise 144,000 Jewish evangelists to take over His witness to the world, as reported in Revelation 7:3–8. They will win a great multitude to Christ in the first three and a half years of the tribulation (Revelation 7:9–17). When the 144,000 Jewish evangelists are raptured in the middle of the tribulation, the task of witnessing to the world, especially the Jewish people, who would then be in the crosshairs of the murderous Antichrist, would fall to the two witnesses/prophets in Revelation 11 for some time. The two witnesses are Enoch and Elijah, who currently stand in the presence of God in their human bodies (Zechariah 4:3, 11–14; Revelation 11:4).

When they finish their testimony, God will lift his protection so the beast out of the bottomless pit (the demonic prince of Grecia (Greece), who will be Satan's executive to assist the Antichrist in his murderous career during the tribulation (Revelation 9:11, 11:7, 13:1–2, 17:8), will kill them, but these will be raptured after three days in the full glare of the world's watching media. After the two prophets are raptured, God will use angels to witness to the world to turn to God and refuse the mark of the beast, which would damn whoever takes it to hell. All these will mean great multitudes will turn to faith in Christ during the tribulation.

During the first three and a half years of the tribulation, believers in Christ (and the Jews) will be murdered by the false church or whore, popularly known as the one world religion, whose beginnings are well under way now, and the ten nations of the revised Roman Empire. It comes in the name of the World Ecumenical Movement, and it seeks to foster cooperation and unity between the religions of the world. Sounds very nice and politically correct, except Christ is not in it.

Many mainline Christian denominations subscribe to this evil, satanic agenda and have been regularly holding 'interfaith services' to foster unity and understanding between religions. The only problem is that it is a Christ-less religious movement or at least not the Jesus of the Bible but some man made Christ who is on the same level as Adam, Abraham, Moses, Ishmael, and God knows who else among the endless list of prophets.

It would be headquatered in Babylon, in Shinar, which God calls the mother of harlots and of the abominations of the earth. Satan has chosen this place as the centre of his activities in the last days to operate against Jerusalem and the Jews. Babylon in Shinar will become the habitation of demons and a hold for every unclean and hated bird (Revelation 2:10, 20:7). It will be the headquarters of the demon world and the concentration of all wickedness. The inhabitants thereof will be spiritists, unclean and vile and possessed by demons, and demon worshippers. It will therefore be the final concentration of martyrdom and reigns of terror.

Revelation 17:6, 18 says, 'I saw the woman, drunk with the blood of the saints and with the martyrs of Jesus.' This speaks of both Jews and Christians being martyred by this beast religion. This false religion will harshly persecute everyone who claims to be born again and who follows any different religion. By this time, the Antichrist has not assumed world prominence, yet he might at best be ruling over one of the nations of the revised Roman Empire (I will show you later which country he will come from, but not now), but he is not yet the world dictator he is soon going to be.

By the end of Revelation 17:16–17, the Antichrist will rise to world prominence after gaining power, first over 1 and then 4 and then (Daniel 7:7–8, 17, *24*) over all ten nations of the revised Roman Empire (at which time he becomes head of his own Grecian Empire, the one that will fight Christ at Armageddon on His second advent) and proceed to destroy the harlot or one world church (Revelation 17: 1, 16–17). His is a political/economic system still based in Babylon and will attempt to kill all believers in Jesus Christ (as these will refuse his mark and expose his lies) and to finally exterminate the Jewish people (Revelation 18:24). Babylon (Shinar) is spiritually under construction for her impending wicked/murderous career (Zechariah 55–11).

> Then one of the elders answered, saying to me, 'Who are these arrayed in white robes, and where did they come from?' And I said to him, 'Sir, you know.'
>
> So he said to me, 'These are the ones who come out of the great tribulation, and washed their robes and made them white in the blood of the Lamb. Therefore they are before the throne of God, and serve Him day and night in His temple. And He who sits on the throne will dwell among them. They shall neither hunger anymore

nor thirst anymore; the sun shall not strike them, nor any heat; for the Lamb who is in the midst of the throne will shepherd them and lead them to living fountains of waters. And God will wipe away every tear from their eyes.'

(Revelation 7:13–17)

And I saw thrones, and they sat upon them, and judgment was given unto them: and I saw the souls of them that were beheaded for the witness of Jesus, and for the word of God, and which had not worshipped the beast, neither his image, neither had received his mark upon their foreheads, or in their hands; and they lived and reigned with Christ a thousand years.

(Revelation 20:4)

Tribulation saints (and the Jews) will go through a horrid and terrible time, with beheadings, rapes, imprisonments, floggings, starvations, tortures, burnings that will make the recent spate of ISIS atrocities in the Middle East seem like child's play. It would engulf most of the world, and most of Europe would not escape. I say this because . . . well, all the murder squads are in place, ready and waiting for the command. These are times like no other.

Not only that, but the appearance of the Antichrist means constant wars (Revelation 6:1–4), famine (Revelation 6:5–6), and death on a scale the world has never witnessed before (Revelation 6:7–8). 'And power was given to them (Death and Hades) over a fourth of the earth, to kill with the sword, with hunger, with death and by the beasts of the earth.' He will attempt to take over the world by conquest and will actually take over most of Asia, (North) Africa, and Europe.

The coming of the *lawless one* is according to the working of Satan, with all power, signs, and lying wonders, and with all unrighteous deception among those who perish, because they did not receive the love of the truth, that

138

they might be saved. And for this reason God will send them strong delusion, that they should believe the lie, that they all may be condemned who did not believe the truth but had pleasure in unrighteousness.

(2 Thessalonians 2:9–12)

During this period, God will permit Satan and his agents to deceive whoever hears but refuses the truth of the gospel to be saved. Revelation 13:13 says God will allow the false prophet to perform great signs so that he even makes fire come down from heaven on the earth in the sight of men and give breath to the image of the beast so that the image is able to speak. All these are to deceive those who have refused the truth of God's saving word to believe the lie of the devil and get them to worship the image of the beast and receive his mark and thereby seal their eternal doom.

Yes, God will counter these deceptions through the ministry of the two witnesses (Elijah and Enoch). The evangelistic work of the tribulation believers who will still be witnessing for Christ under very dangerous circumstances (that and refusing the mark of the beast) is what gets many of them martyred. Many Jewish people will also come to faith during this time and would be witnessing for Christ, the ministry of the three angels who will preach the gospel and warn earth dwellers about the mark, and of course, the continuing ministry of the Holy Spirit.

So God will continue to be faithful in warning people about the deceptions of the devil and his agents, but He will permit the deceptions, nonetheless. That is why it is dangerous to delay your decision about Christ. God has not promised tomorrow to anybody. He says today if you will hear His voice, do not harden your heart, for tomorrow may be too late. It is not a risk worth taking. Heaven is real, and so is hell. So I will encourage you not to leave for tomorrow what you should do today. Give your life to Jesus, and avoid a painful regret tomorrow. The rich man in the story of Luke 16:19–31 prayed for Abraham to send somebody from the dead to tell his five brothers about the truth and reality of hell because 'if one goes to them from the dead, they will repent'.

Well, Jesus went to Hades, or hell, and came back to tell the horrors of the place and warned people against going there. Jesus spoke about hell and the horrors of the place and offered us the way to avoid going there. If you end up there, it will be by your own will and choice. You may be saying, 'I don't believe in this hell thing.' Fine, that is still your choice, but your believing or not believing will not change a thing. It is waiting, patiently, for you. It has been there even before your great-great-great-grandmother was born. You may hang around here a hundred years, fine, but hell has got all the patience in the world, knowing that if you refuse Christ, you cannot escape its clutches. Run for your life, and do it now.

During this period of tribulation, God will literally remove his restraint over the animal kingdom so that wild beasts from the jungle and the seas and the skies will invade the earth to attack and kill humans. This removal of His restraint will also apply to the demonic world, which would actually be living right on the earth, as opposed to the second heavens, where they are now. And these demented, merciless demonic creatures will wreak havoc on mankind (Revelation 12:8, 9, 12; 18:1–2; 6:8b). Sheer criminality and lawlessness will take over many nations of the world as the Antichrist's spirit, who is also called the lawless one, sweeps over the world. It is only the Lord's protection which is covering His children in the world today. You know as well as I that if they had their way, we would be out of their way, as they hate the very name we profess.

Revelation 9:21 says, 'And they did not repent of their murders, or their sorceries (witchcraft, magic and drugs), or their sexual immorality or their thefts.'

It is actually a blessing to be martyred during the tribulation (Revelation 14:13) as this gives one the chance to be raptured and become a part of the first resurrection (Revelation 20:4–6). But God in His mercy has indicated clearly that the great tribulation and the persecution will only last 1,260 from the time the Antichrist enters the rebuilt temple in Jerusalem till he is defeated at Armageddon. So the suffering is not forever. Yes, some believers would escape death and survive on earth till Christ comes to rescue them, but they will still go through a terrible time hiding from the Antichrist's mob squads. That is why the Bible admonishes us all: 'Today if you will hear His voice, do not harden your hearts.' Isaiah 55:6 says 'Seek the Lord, while He may be found, Call upon Him while He is near.'

You can accept Jesus as your Lord and Saviour by saying this simple prayer and by believing in Him in your heart: 'Lord Jesus, I acknowledge that I am a sinner. I believe you are the Son of God and that you died on the cross for my sins. I now invite you into my heart to be my Lord and Saviour. Thank you for saving my soul. Amen' (Romans 10:9–11, 13). After saying this prayer, you are born again. You need to find a church which will teach you the Word of God so you can grow in your new faith.

ALL YOU NEED TO KNOW
ABOUT THE ANTICHRIST

Who is the Antichrist, also known as the beast out of the sea (Revelation 13:1–6, 6:1–2)?

The beast symbolises *three things* in scripture.

The beast in Revelation refers to the rise of a kingdom or the earthly head of that kingdom, such as the king or emperor or the supernatural, demonic spirit that rules over that kingdom. So in this instance, the Antichrist is the human head of the revived Grecian Empire (Revelation 13:1–5; 17:8), and the supernatural being is the beast (the demonic prince) out of the abyss (Revelation 11:7, 17; 17:8; 19:19–21; 20; 10). The empire here is the eighth kingdom, which immediately succeeds the seven heads or kingdoms, which is the revived Grecian Empire (Revelation 13:1; 17:3, 7–11; Daniel 7:7, 8, 19–25).

WHO IS HE?

The antichrist is a real person, a human being, yet to come in the future to fulfil all the Bible prophecies concerning him (see his titles below). He will possess great leadership talents and natural gifts and miraculous powers to attract all classes of people, fascinating them with his marvellous personality, prowess, wisdom, and administrative and executive abilities. He will be a master diplomat and will bring people under his spell with masterly flattery and diplomacy and will be a great military strategist. He will be endowed with the power of Satan in the exercise of these gifts and will hold the world spellbound until many worship him as god. From the time he is revealed in Revelation 6:2, he goes out conquering and to conquer. His reign is marked by wars, worldwide carnage, famine, and death on a global scale.

No one knows who the Antichrist is at the present time. It is not possible to know, as the scripture does not reveal who he is until after he personally makes a seven-year covenant of peace with unbelieving Israel (Daniel 7:27). God gave the prophet Daniel a series of visions (some to King Nebuchadnezzar) in which He revealed all the Gentile nations that have persecuted and will continue to persecute Israel throughout the times of the Gentiles, from Babylon to Medo-Persia, Greece, ancient Rome, revised Rome, and finally, the revived Grecian Empire, which will be the eighth and final empire that will lead the armies of the Antichrist to fight Christ on His Second Coming at the battle of Armageddon. Daniel did not see the first two empires that persecuted Israel in his visions, as she had specifically prayed to know what will happen to his people in the future, but these actually started with Egypt and Assyria. The last two empires, revised Rome and revived Greece, are still in the future but would make their appearance on the world stage soon, in order. All these empires will be in the revised Roman Empire and thence the revived Grecian Empire, over which the Antichrist would rule.

In his vision in Daniel 7:7, 8, 20, Daniel saw a dreadful and terrible beast with ten horns, and then another horn, a little one, comes up among them. Then three of the ten horns were plucked out by the roots. The beast is the revised Roman Empire. The ten horns are the ten constituent nations or the leaders thereof. The little horn that comes up among the ten is the Antichrist. It means that by the beginning of the seven-year tribulation, the Antichrist would emerge out of the eastern wing of the revised Roman Empire.

In Daniel 7:23–24, it says the fourth beast shall be the fourth kingdom on the earth (Babylon, Medo-Persia, Greece, and then the Roman Empire) which shall be diverse from all kingdoms. The ten horns out of this kingdom (Rome) are ten kings that shall arise. Then *another* shall arise *after* them, and he shall be diverse from the first and shall subdue three kings.

Interpretation: When the revised Roman Empire appears on the world stage, the Antichrist would be the leader of one of the ten kingdoms. Remember, Daniel saw Rome as two legs of iron and later as ten toes on the two feet. The Roman Empire has an eastern division and a western division. Some of the key nations in the eastern division include Egypt, Turkey, and Syria. At the beginning of the seven-year tribulation, he will be the leader of just one of these countries, but by the middle of the tribulation (after three and a half years), he will overthrow three of these ten nations—namely, Greece, Egypt, and Turkey. After gaining control of four out of ten of these nations, the remaining six will agree to give their power to him; thus, he will have control of all ten nations and go on to form his own empire, the eighth and final, the Grecian Empire.

The moment he gains control of the four key Grecian nations, which were also in the Roman Empire, his empire ceases to be Roman and becomes Grecian (Daniel 10:20). The Antichrist will be backed by a mighty supernatural satanic power that the book of Revelation calls the beast out of the abyss, who was the ruling principality of the old Grecian Empire and was confined to the abyss or the bottomless pit after Greece fell. This powerful demonic prince will be released from the bottomless pit at the beginning of the tribulation, revive the Grecian Empire, and it is he who will help the Antichrist rise to power (Revelation 13:1–3; Revelation 9:1–11). It is clear that this 'little horn' arises *after* the ten kingdoms and not *before* them (Daniel 10:20, 11:1–3).

Daniel 8 is a vision about Medo-Persia (the ram with two horns) and Greece (the he goat with a notable horn), which succeeds Medo-Persia. Daniel 8:8 says that when the male goat grew very strong, the large horn was broken and, in its place, grew four notable horns. The large horn is Alexander the Great, who founded the Grecian Empire. When he died at a young age, at the height of his power, his empire was broken into four among his four top generals. These four divisions were Syria, Turkey, Egypt, and Greece. Daniel 8:23 says in the latter time of their kingdom (when Greece is revived at the end times), a king shall arise, having fierce features, who understands sinister schemes. This is none other than the Antichrist, who will emerge from either Greece,

Egypt, Turkey, or Syria. It is stated that 'the little horn' will come out of one of the four horns: 'Out of one of them came a little horn.' Daniel 8 narrows the ten kingdoms of the revived Roman Empire of Daniel 7 to four kingdoms from which the Antichrist could come, which are either Greece, Turkey, Syria, or Egypt. Of these fouir kingdoms, Syria and Egypt are the ones that historically persecuted the Jewish people and hence prophetically relevant here.

Then in Daniel 11, we have an account of protracted wars between two of the four divisions of the Grecian Empire, Egypt (the king of the south), and Syria (the king of the north) for over one hundred fifty years. Then the prophet says there are going to be wars in the end time between these two nations in which Syria ultimately defeats Egypt (Daniel 11:40–45) to show that the Antichrist would come from Syria.

WHEN WILL HE BE REVEALED?

1. After the ten kingdoms are formed in the old Roman Empire territory (Daniel 7:24; Revelation 13:2–4, 17:12–17).
2. After the rapture of the church (2 Thessalonians 2:6–8). The church, through the indwelling of the omnipotent Holy Spirit, is the restrainer of the Antichrist. So Spirit-indwelt Christians must first be removed from the earth before the Antichrist can show up. So God is holding back the Antichrist through the presence of Christians on the earth.
3. After he signs the seven-year (peace) treaty with unbelieving Israel (Daniel 9:27).

Interestingly, in Revelation 6:1–2, when the lamb opens one of the seals, one of the four living creatures had to say 'Come' before the rider on the white horse, the Antichrist, comes on to the world stage. *The Antichrist can only show up in his office at the express permission of the Lord Jesus Christ.* Until this time, it is impossible to know his identity, and all speculation about his identity is bound to fail. Please understand that there is a difference between the spirit of the Antichrist and the

Antichrist. The spirit of Antichrist, the Bible says, has been in the world even since Christ's day. It is simply the spirit of lawlessness, of which the Bible says there are many already in the world.

It is that spirit that took over the Jerusalem mob to shout 'Crucify Him! Crucify Him!' on the day Jesus was crucified. Many of these same crowd were people Jesus had healed and fed only days earlier, but when that spirit swept over them, the same people were saying 'We have no king but Caesar' and 'His blood be on us and on our children'. Did you witness the atrocities and mass murder of ISIS and others that fly planes into buildings to kill as many people as possible? That is the spirit of the Antichrist at work, the spirit that denies the relationship between the Father and the Son and says that God has no Son and that Jesus is not the Son of God and that He did not die on the cross and neither did He rise from the dead. It denies the very deity of Jesus.

That spirit undermines everything that is Christian and the Bible. It is the spirit of Islam. Islam is a Christian cult, just like Mormonism and the JWs. They have all come to persecute the church. Jesus said that a time is coming that 'whoever kills you would think he offers God a service'. And sure enough, they are killing in the name of God (John 16:2). The unbelieving world clearly tolerates this spirit because the whole world is under the sway of the evil one. The spirit of the Antichrist has the task of preparing the minds and hearts of the world for the arrival of the Antichrist so that when the true believers in Jesus are removed out of the way, the Antichrist and his false prophet would be readily accepted by most of the people of the world without question.

Recently, I was watching television showing the aftermath of a major disaster and how different groups of people were all pulling their efforts in helping the victims. I must admit, it was beautiful, and the world needs more of such collaboration. Then an elderly lady stepped forward to be interviewed, and she mentioned her particular religious affiliation and added that this is what religion is all about, working together to alleviate the suffering of mankind because, at the end of the day, 'We are all serving the same god.' Isn't that sweet? But there goes the deception: 'We serve the same god.' If that were true, why would that god mandate his followers to behead people of other faiths for failing to convert? Have you noticed that there is an inherent hatred for Christianity and Christians in most nations, even including so-called Christian nations, that is a manifestation of that spirit?

But the Antichrist is a person, a human being, who would be empowered by Satan and his demons and would be the most vile, wicked, and murderous human that ever lived. He is also known as the son of perdition because he is headed for destruction. He has not shown up yet but could be waiting in the wings, somewhere, maybe without knowing he is the one.

THE ANTICHRIST IS ALWAYS BLASPHEMING GOD

Daniel 11:36–39 says that he shall exalt and magnify himself above every god, shall speak blasphemies against the God of Gods, and shall regard neither the God of his fathers nor the desire of women. Remember that Muslims of the Middle East descended from Abraham through Ishmael and Esau.

Daniel 7:8b says that there in this horn (the little horn or the Antichrist) were eyes like the eyes of a man and a mouth speaking pompous words, and he shall speak pompous words against the Most High.

Revelation 13:5–6 says, 'And he was given a mouth speaking great things and blasphemies . . . and he opened his mouth in blasphemy against God, to blaspheme His name, His tabernacle, and those who dwell in heaven.' Historically, all the kings and emperors of all the six historical empires that have oppressed Israel in the past have been blasphemous. Some have actually declared themselves as a god and demanded to be worshipped. The closest we come to the Antichrist in history is Antiochus Epiphanes, who ruled the Celucian Empire, which comprised Turkey, Syria, Iraq, Iran, Lebanon (the northern power base or the king of the north) from 175 to 164 BC. He was called god in the flesh. Antiochus desecrated the temple in Jerusalem in 168 BC. The Antichrist would be no different.

He cannot be bothered about women's rights or feelings. He is anti women's rights and a great persecutor of women. Sharia is anti women, and you know who is behind it. Following Genesis 3:15, when God said, 'I will put enmity between you and the woman, and between your seed and her seed,' the devil clearly understood that this prophesied the virgin birth of the Messiah and has been persecuting and oppressing women ever since. The devil's seed here refers to his servants.

HOW LONG WILL HE REIGN?

1. Over one of the ten kingdoms of revised Rome, at the beginning of the week, but over all ten kingdoms, by the middle of the week. Even though each of these nations would have a national leader, they will all be subject to his supreme will (Revelation 13:5; Daniel 7:25, 12:7). It is during the last three and a half years that he will exalt himself above every god to be worshipped as god (Revelation 13:4–18; Daniel 8:25, 11:36–45; 2 Thessalonians 2:4).
2. He will first rule from rebuilt Babylon and then from Jerusalem 'in the glorious holy mountain' during part of the last three and a half years (Daniel 11:45; 2 Thessalonians 2:4; Daniel 9:27; 12:7–13, 8:13; Matthew 24:15–22; Revelation 11:1–2).

THE SOURCE OF THE ANTICHRIST'S POWER

1. Satan (Daniel 8:24; 2 Thessalonians 2:8–12; Revelation 13:1–2)
2. The spirit from the abyss who would be Satan's executive demonic agent assigned to the Antichrist, the prince of Grecia (Revelation 11:7; 17:8, 11)
3. The ten kings of revised Rome (Revelation 17:12–17).

His power has been decreed by God to be given him.

He will succeed in his world conquest by conquering revised Rome by the middle of the week and all the northern and eastern countries of Europe and Asia by the end of the week (Daniel 11:40–44). He will get the cooperation of many other nations through the ministry of the three unclean froglike spirits (Revelation 16:13–14).

After his defeat at Armageddon by Christ and his heavenly armies, he will be cast into the lake of fire, where he will be tormented forever (Revelation 19:19–20).

HIS TITLES

Some of his titles reveal the countries he will rule over:

1. Antichrist (1 John 2:18, 22, 4:3; 2 John 7)
2. The Assyrian (Isaiah 10:20–27, 30:18–33, 31:4–32; Micah 5:3–15)
3. The king of Babylon (Isaiah 14:4, 13:6–16)
4. The spoiler and the extortionist (Isaiah 16:1–5)
5. Gog, the chief prince of Meshech and Tubal (in Turkey) (Ezekiel 38–39)
6. The little horn (Daniel 7:8, 24; 8:9, 23)
7. A king of fierce countenance (Daniel 8:23)
8. The prince that shall come (Daniel 9:26–27)
9. The king of the north (Syria) (Daniel 11:36–45)
10. The man of sin (2 Thessalonians 2:1–12)
11. The son of perdition (2 Thessalonians 2:1–12)
12. The wicked and that wicked (Isaiah 11:4; 2 Thessalonians 2:1–12)
13. The king of Tyre (in Lebanon)
14. The beast (Daniel 7:11; Revelation 13:1–18, 14:9–11)
15. Pharaoh, king of Egypt (Ezekiel 32:31).

THE EXTENT OF HIS REIGN (REVELATION 13:7–10)

The Antichrist will not rule over the whole world, even though that will be his ambition, but he will be stopped by Christ before he comes anywhere close. His empire would cover the southern part of Europe, the western part of Asia, and the northern parts of Africa. This does not mean that his influence could not be felt way beyond his political domain. In addition, he will introduce his mark of the beast at the beginning of the last three and a half years, but he will not have time to enforce it all over the world. It is the Antichrist who introduces the mark in the middle of the week, so all talk about the mark today is futile speculation, even though the technology may well be available in the world today. Besides, like any law, there will be several ways to evade it, and many people will be able to do just that, even within the ten kingdoms directly under his rule. For instance, Zechariah records that everyone who is left of all nations which came against Jerusalem shall go up from year to year to worship the King, the Lord of Hosts . . . and if the family of Egypt will not come and enter in, they shall have no rain (14:16, 18).

If he ruled the whole world, he would not need the ministry of the three demonic froglike spirits to seek the cooperation of the rulers of the nations to join him in his battle with Christ at Armageddon (Revelation 16:13).

Also, if all nations were to cooperate with the Antichrist for the destruction of Israel, there would be no sheep nations to enter the millennium under Christ (Matthew 24–25). However, the tribulation would be such an awful time on earth that no sane human should be looking forward to it.

As a Christian, you may know about him from the scriptures but not meet him in person, so focus on living for Christ, because you will depart to keep a crucial appointment with the Lord of Glory before he shows up (Isaiah 26:20–21).

Friend, the Word of God is so true. What I am teaching you here is the pure Word, plain and simple. With all humility, an anointed teacher stays close to the text of scripture without any exaggeration and fanciful speculative interpretations. In Daniel 12:4, 9 and 8:26b, 'And he said, "Go your way, Daniel, for the words are closed up and sealed till the time of the end."' The clear implication is that as we approach the time of the end, we shall understand the so-called hitherto difficult scriptures, such as the books of Daniel and Revelation (Isaiah 11:1–2). I am saying this so that you will open up to understand these great end-time mysteries that God in His abundant grace has enabled us to understand. All the glory goes to Him and the wonderful Holy Spirit, the greatest author and teacher there ever was. Like He did to Daniel, may He give you skill to understand. Amen.

WARS OF THE ANTICHRIST

The Antichrist is a man of war and will be fighting from the day he makes his debut on the world stage. Daniel 11:38 says he shall honour a god of fortresses. He is not an atheist, but his religion would believe in warfare. This is clearly Islam, the religion of war. Revelation 6:2 says, 'And I looked and behold, a white horse. He who sat on it had a bow; and a crown was given to him, and he went out conquering and to conquer.' In fact, the very first thing he does to establish his credentials would be to overthrow three nations within the revised Roman Empire. Daniel 7:24 says, 'The ten horns are 10 kings who shall arise from this kingdom. And another shall arise after them [the Antichrist] and he shall be different from the first ones, and shall subdue three kings [i.e. Turkey, Greece and Egypt].'

After the Jewish people rebel against his authority and refuse to worship him as God following the abomination of desolation (the desecration of the Jewish temple), he will become their most bitter enemy and will launch a campaign to exterminate them from the middle of the week. Daniel 8:24b says he shall destroy the mighty and also the holy people (Israel). Micah 5:5–6 says that the Assyrian, another name for the Antichrist, will enter the land of Israel but God will raise seven shepherds and eight princely men to deliver Israel from his hand. This coalition of seven shepherds and eight princely men may well be a coalition of America and her allies, who would boot the Antichrist and his forces out of Israel (Ezekiel 28:7). Daniel 11:41 says he shall enter the glorious land and many countries shall be overthrown but these shall escape from his hand: Edom, Moab, and the prominent people of Ammon. This is repeated in Revelation 12:6, 13–14, in which the believing Jews flee to Petra in Jordan, where God will hide them for the rest of the tribulation. It is possible Israel would be ruling over Jordan following her victory in the Psalm 83 war, so it would be easy for the Jews to flee there. The Antichrist would not pursue them into Jordan but would return to devastate the Jewish mainland, Judea and Samaria.

Daniel 11:39 actually says he shall act against the strongest fortresses with a foreign god and this may well be when he invades Israel and America and her allies intervene to boot her out.

Daniel 11:42–43 says he shall stretch out his hand against the countries and the land of Egypt shall not escape and also the Libyans and Ethiopians (possibly Sudan translated from Cush) shall follow at his heels. In verse 44, news from the east (possibly Far Eastern countries) and north (possibly northern European nations) shall trouble him, so he will go out with great fury to destroy and annihilate many.

The Antichrist will also use skilled diplomacy, deception, and bribery (Daniel 11:21, 23–24) to bring nations under his authority. He shall come in peaceably and seize the kingdom by intrigue after the league is made with him. He shall act deceitfully. He shall enter peaceably and shall disperse among them the plunder, spoil and riches . . . He is a master deceiver.

2 Thessalonians says that the coming of the lawless one is according to the working of Satan, with all power, signs, lying wonders, and all unrighteous deception among those who perish, because they did not receive the love of the truth that they may be saved.

He will also use the ministry of the three froglike spirits to get nations to cooperate with him in his wars and murderous schemes (Revelation 16:13–14). Certainly, these demons would be instrumental in gathering the nations that are not directly under his rule to the battle of Armageddon to face Jesus Christ and His heavenly army. This would be a step too far for the Antichrist and his forces because they will be consumed with the breath of His mouth and destroyed with the brightness of His coming by Christ. (Joel 2:20–21). The northern army refers to Syria, the king of the north. He will be destroyed at Armageddon in Israel and thrown into the lake of fire with his false prophet (Isaiah 11:45; 2 Thessalonians 2:8).

HIS END IS SURE TO COME

> And I saw an angel standing in the sun, who cried in a loud voice to all the birds flying in midair, 'Come, gather together for the great supper of God, so that you may eat the flesh of kings, generals, and the mighty, of horses and their riders, and the flesh of all people, free and slave, great and small.'
>
> Then I saw the beast and the kings of the earth and their armies gathered together to wage war against the rider on the horse and his army. But the beast was captured, and with it the false prophet who had performed the signs on its behalf. With these signs he had deluded those who had received the mark of the beast and worshiped its image. The two of them were thrown alive into the fiery lake of burning sulfur. The rest were killed with the sword coming out of the mouth of the rider on the horse, and all the birds gorged themselves on their flesh.
>
> (Revelation 19:17–21, NIV)

The Antichrist, like most world dictators, by demonic power would attempt to rule the whole world but would fail and come to his ignominious end. He would be so deluded and deceived as to want to fight Christ at His advent at Armageddon, but Christ is Lord of

Lords and King of Kings, the one and only Potentate, the head of all principality and power. Psalm 2:1–2 says the nations rage and the peoples plot a vain thing and the kings of the earth set themselves and the rulers take counsel together against the Lord and against His anointed, saying, 'Let us break their bonds in pieces and cast away their cords from us.'

But what is God's response to them? He laughs at them and holds them in derision, because they are no match for Him.

Do not be afraid of the Antichrist and all the rumours circulating about him. He cannot show up on the earth until Christ lets him. And before He lets him in, He is sure to take you out of here to the comfort of His presence in heaven. He is faithful in delivering His children from the wrath to come (1 Thessalonians 1:10b), because He did not appoint us to wrath but to obtain salvation through our Lord Jesus Christ, who died for us that whether we wake or sleep, we should live together with Him.

Just focus on living for Christ. Get busy in His vineyard, telling others about His saving love for them and the provision He has already made for their salvation. And the Antichrist will not so much as set his eye on you.

I invite you to accept Jesus as your Lord and Saviour by saying this simple prayer and to believe in Him in your heart. You see, you can only go to heaven by trusting Christ to take you there. He is the only one that can: 'Lord Jesus, I acknowledge that I am a sinner. I believe You are the Son of God and that You died on the cross for my sins. I now invite You into my heart to be my Lord and Saviour. Thank You for saving my soul. Amen.' After saying this prayer, you are born again. You need to find a church which will teach you the Word of God so you can grow in your new faith.

THE BEAST OUT OF THE ABYSS—THE PRINCE OF GRECIA (REVELATION 11:7; 17:7, 8; LUKE 8:31)

The abyss, also known as the bottomless pit, is a prison for demon spirits. It is also a place where certain satanic princes have been shut up and confined. Those spirits do not have the freedom to roam the earth. Similarly, Peter says in 2 Peter 2:4, 'For if God did not spare the angels who sinned, but cast them down to hell and delivered them in into chains of darkness to be reserved for judgement.' Jude also says in verse 6, 'And the angels who did not keep their proper domain, but left their own abode, He has reserved in everlasting chains in darkness for the judgement of the great day.'

From the above scriptures, we understand that some demonic princes and demons have been imprisoned or confined to certain places by God to be brought up for judgement at the great white throne judgement or the final judgement at the end of the millennial kingdom of Christ. The abyss, or the bottomless pit, is one such prison for evil spirits. No human goes there. The souls of all dead humans who do not know Christ as Lord and Saviour go to hell, the holding prison for humans.

Before the resurrection of Christ from the dead, all departed human souls, the righteous and the unjust, went to hell, which was divided into two—one part for the righteous, called Abraham's bosom, and the hell proper. These two places were separated by a great chasm, and even though you could see one part from the other, it was not possible to cross from one side to the other because of the great chasm (Luke 16:19–31; Psalm 16:10; Luke 23:43; Revelation 20:11–15). When Christ rose from the dead, He took the righteous souls from paradise, or Abraham's bosom, and they too went with Him to heaven. From that time on, all righteous souls go straight to heaven to be with Christ until the first resurrection when we shall all receive our immortal human bodies fit for all eternity (Ephesians 4:7–11; Hebrews 2:14; Philippians 1:21; 2 Corinthians 5:8; Revelation 6:9–11). Sadly, hell has enlarged itself to occupy the place that formally held the righteous people, because of the sheer numbers of people pouring into hell.

According to Revelation 20:1–10, the abyss will be Satan's prison for a thousand years, following his defeat and capture at the battle of Armageddon. He will be captured and chained and thrown down into the abyss. So it is clear from these scriptures that the abyss is reserved as a prison for Satan and his demons and his angelic spirits, but never for humans.

SO WHO IS THIS BEAST OUT OF THE ABYSS?

We believe this beast is a mighty supernatural satanic prince, who would be working under Satan to dominate and support the Antichrist as the earthly king over the last and final earthly kingdom, the revived empire of Greece, at the end of this age. This satanic ruler must have ruled one of the first five empires which preceded John's day. These are represented by the first five heads on the beast. When his empire fell to make way for the sixth kingdom of old Rome, this satanic prince was cast into and confined in the abyss. So this prince, though alive, was not on the earth during John's day—that is, at the time of old Rome. This prince would be confined in his prison until the formation of the ten kingdoms of revised Rome as the seventh world empire. Immediately after the formation of the seventh world empire, He will be released from his prison and will engineer the rise of the Antichrist out of the ten kingdoms. The Antichrist will be the leader of one of these ten nations, but this spirit will help him supernaturally to subdue three kings of the ten nations and help him revive the empire of Greece, which he ruled before he was confined to the abyss. So the empire which this demonic prince ruled before, the Grecian Empire, would be revived to be the last world empire, which the Antichrist will rule and which will fight Christ on His return at the battle of Armageddon.

This is what the angel meant here:

> The beast that you saw was, and is not, and will ascend
> out of the bottomless pit and go to perdition. And those
> who dwell on the earth will marvel, whose names are

not written in the Book of Life from the foundation of the world, when they see the beast that was, and is not, and yet is.

The beast that was, and is not, is himself also the eighth, and is of the 7, and is going to perdition

When they finish their testimony, the beast that ascends out of the bottomless pit will make war against them, overcome them and kill them.

(Revelation 17:8, 11, 11:7)

The fifth angel sounded his trumpet, and I saw a star that had fallen from the sky to the earth. The star was given the key to the shaft of the Abyss. [2] When he opened the Abyss, smoke rose from it like the smoke from a gigantic furnace. The sun and sky were darkened by the smoke from the Abyss.

(Revelation 9:1–2, 11)

They had as king over them the angel of the abyss, whose name in Hebrew is Abaddon and in Greek is Apollyon (that is, 'destroyer').

This is what the angel meant in Revelation 17: 8 when he said the beast *was* (meaning had existed on earth before John's time) and is not (on the earth during John's day) and shall ascend out of the bottomless pit (in the last day to revive the kingdom he ruled before he was incarcerated in the abyss) and go to perdition or be destroyed or go into the lake of fire. This mighty demonic prince will control the Antichrist through demons and all kinds of evil spirits and thus make him the embodiment of all evil and wickedness and the utter manifestation of satanic power.

This is the symbol of the beast out of the abyss, who will orchestrate the rise of the Antichrist (the beast out of the sea of humanity) to revive and form the beast (the eighth kingdom), which is revived Grecia. All these three are symbolised by the beast. In Revelation 11:7, this beast out of the abyss makes war on the two witnesses after they have finished their prophecy and kills them through the Antichrist.

The kingdoms of this world have always been controlled by supernatural demonic powers, and what happens in the natural realm has always been dictated by what happens in the heavenlies, the results of the battles lost or won between the forces of God and those of Satan.

> So he said, 'Do you know why I have come to you? Soon I will return to fight against the prince of Persia, and when I go, the prince of Greece will come; but first I will tell you what is written in the Book of Truth. (No one supports me against them except Michael, your prince. And in the first year of Darius the Mede, I took my stand to support and protect him.)
>
> 'Now then, I tell you the truth: Three more kings will arise in Persia, and then a fourth, who will be far richer than all the others. When he has gained power by his wealth, he will stir up everyone against the kingdom of Greece.'
>
> (Daniel 10:20–11:2)

The devil controls the kingdoms of this world. This is the result of Adam's high treason. He offered it to Jesus in exchange for the latter to worship him.

> Then the devil, taking Him up on a high mountain, showed Him all the kingdoms of the world in a moment of time. And the devil said to Him, 'All this authority I will give You, and their glory; for *this* has been delivered to me, and I give it to whomever I wish.
>
> (Luke 4:5–6)

At this time, God interferes with and disrupts the plans of Satan in the kingdoms of this world to enable His prophetic word to be fulfilled, which Satan and his demons are working around the clock to thwart and cause to fail, hence the constant, almost nonstop war in the heavenlies. These battles between Satan and his forces on one hand and God and His forces on the other can be traced all through the Bible from Genesis to Revelation as God seeks to restore man to his position before the fall. In the Old Testament, it was the coming of the seed of the woman and the fulfilment of God's purposes concerning Israel.

According the Genesis 3:15 prophecy:

> And I will put enmity
> Between you and the woman,
> And between your seed and her Seed;
> He shall bruise your head,
> And you shall bruise His heel.

In fact, this is the reason God has asked His children, the Christians, in Genesis 12:1–3, to specifically pray for Israel and promised an incentive, a blessing, with it. He knew that because of the prophetic destiny of the Jewish people, they will be the target of Satanic onslaught all through history. How true this has proven all through the ages, right from the day God called Abraham and promised to raise a prophetic and evangelistic nation through them and use them as his conduit for reaching the rest of humanity. It is instructive to know that all of God's blessings for Gentiles come through the Jews—from the Word of God and the enriching promises therein to the prophets and patriarchs that we also claim as our fathers and to His ultimate blessing to mankind, the Lord Jesus Christ, the Son of Man, who was Himself Jewish according to His human heritage. However, God uses the Gentiles to chastise, discipline, or punish Israel, but he punishes and disciplines Gentiles directly.

Even humanly speaking, tiny Israel today has continues to be a blessing to all mankind in a way grossly out of proportion to their numerical strength in fields of agriculture, technology, science, economics, innovation, medicine, and every other conceivable field of human development.

> Concerning His Son Jesus Christ our Lord, who was born of the seed of David according to the flesh.
>
> (Romans 1:3)

> Now the LORD had said to Abram:
> 'Get out of your country,
> From your family
> And from your father's house,
> To a land that I will show you.
> I will make you a great nation;
> I will bless you
> And make your name great;
> And you shall be a blessing.
> I will bless those who bless you,
> And I will curse him who curses you;
> And in you all the families of the earth shall be blessed.'
>
> (Genesis 12:1–3)

The number-one weapon used by the devil in his bid to destroy Israel and wipe them from the face of the earth till today has been the kingdoms of this world.

Prayer to Frustrate Conspiracy Against Israel
A Song. A Psalm of Asaph.
83 Do not keep silent, O God!
Do not hold Your peace,
And do not be still, O God!
For behold, Your enemies make a tumult;
And those who hate You have lifted up their head.
They have taken crafty counsel against Your people,
And consulted together against Your sheltered ones.

They have said, 'Come, and let us cut them off from
being a nation,
That the name of Israel may be remembered no more.'
For they have consulted together with one consent;
They form a confederacy against You:
The tents of Edom and the Ishmaelites;
Moab and the Hagrites;
Gebal, Ammon, and Amalek;
Philistia with the inhabitants of Tyre;
Assyria also has joined with them;
They have helped the children of Lot. Selah.

(Psalm 83:1–8)

All these is a satanic bid to destroy Israel and the Jewish people from the face of the earth because of the prophetic destiny they carry and the crucial role they have been allotted in God's redemption programme for man.

From the very beginning of Israel's history, in Genesis 12 throughout the Old Testament, there were five great kingdoms that Satan had used to try to destroy Israel, i.e. Egypt, Assyria, Babylon, Medo-Persia, Greece (the fifth that had already fallen before John). The sixth was the old Roman Empire, which existed at the time of John. All these six empires are now historical. They have all persecuted Israel when they ruled much of the ancient world. The seventh empire will be a revision of the sixth, the Roman Empire in the form of ten kingdoms within the territory of the old Roman Empire. This will have an eastern wing and a western wing and will also persecute Israel. This will exist for a short space of time only before it is succeeded by the eighth, the beast, or the Grecian Empire, the empire of the Antichrist, destined to be the most bitter persecutor of Israel. For the three and a half years that this empire will be on the world stage, it will try to carry out Satan's original plan to destroy and exterminate the Jews completely and thereby thwart God's eternal plan and purpose for the nation and the world.

In Daniel 10:20–11:2, we have the pivotal passage in all the Bible concerning the supernatural princes under Satan who rule over different kingdoms and nations of the earth.

> So he said, 'Do you know why I have come to you? Soon I will return to fight against the prince of Persia, and when I go, the prince of Greece will come; but first I will tell you what is written in the Book of Truth. (No one supports me against them except Michael, your prince. And in the first year of Darius the Mede, I took my stand to support and protect him.)

The Kings of the South and the North

> Now then, I tell you the truth: Three more kings will arise in Persia, and then a fourth, who will be far richer than all the others. When he has gained power by his wealth, he will stir up everyone against the kingdom of Greece.

Gabriel is saying it was he who helped Darius, the Mede, to come to power by defeating the principality over Babylon in the heavenlies, the preceding empire. That explains why the Babylonian Empire fell so easily to the Medo-Persia. He is saying that the time for Medo-Persia is almost over and that Greece would be taking over—that was why the prince of Grecia would be showing forth soon after Medo-Persia. When Greece also fell to the Romans, it meant the prince of Greece, who is the beast out of the abyss, whose name is Abaddon or Apollyon, was defeated in the heavenlies for the ruling prince of Rome to take over. This explains why the spirit in the abyss was confined there in the bottomless pit.

This is what the angel meant in Revelation 17 when he said the beast *was* (meaning had existed on earth before John's time) and is not (on the earth during John's day), and shall ascend out of the bottomless pit (in the last day to revive the kingdom he ruled before he was incarcerated in the abyss).

He was on the earth before the sixth and was not on the earth during the sixth. He will come out of the abyss during the seventh; revive the kingdom he once ruled, Greece, to become the eighth; be defeated at Armageddon; and be cast into the lake of fire for ever and be destroyed. This is clear proof of the control of supernatural powers over kingdoms, all kingdoms, not just those mentioned in the Bible. That is why God asks His children to pray for kings and rulers and people with authority over nations.

> I urge, then, first of all, that petitions, prayers, intercession and thanksgiving be made for all people— for kings and all those in authority, that we may live peaceful and quiet lives in all godliness and holiness.
>
> (1 Timothy 2:1–2)

This is what opens the door for God to influence the lives and decisions of national leaders; otherwise, they are at the mercy of the ruling demonic principalities over their nation. In fact, major towns and cities also have spirits that rule over them to influence the lives and character of the inhabitants thereof. A careful observation would easily reveal the nature of the ruling powers over a nation, region, or town by looking at the dominant character of the inhabitants. Some of these could be religious spirits, spirits of mammon, bloodshed, murder, immorality, alcoholism, perverted sexual behaviours, and the like.

Many people have reported that prayer is a struggle in certain places and countries than others. Several years ago, I was travelling with a pastor friend of mine in Accra, Ghana, and as we crossed from one street to the other side of the same street, I noticed a sudden change in the atmosphere. I blurted out to my friend that the air feels different on this side, and the friend remarked that it was true because the people that lived on the other side were of a particular religion, different from those on the other side. This control of territories and nations by the forces of darkness will continue until the kingdoms of this world become the kingdoms of our God and of His Christ.

> Then the seventh angel sounded: And there were loud voices in heaven, saying, 'The kingdoms of this world have become the kingdoms of our Lord and of His Christ, and He shall reign forever and ever!'
>
> (Revelation 11:15)

Until that time, we are called to contain the influence of these satanic forces by praying for our nations and their leaders.

The angel Gabriel said he was the angel used by God to strengthen King Darius, the Mede, so that the prince of Persia might come to power, who was to deliver Israel and permit them to return to their own land. In the spirit realm, the prince is the ruling spirit over a nation or kingdom who directly reports to Satan and is higher than the king. We can safely conclude that the beast is the spirit of Grecia because the body of the beast is 'like a leopard', which symbolises the Grecian Empire. In Daniel's vision:

> Then I stood on the sand of the sea. And I saw a beast rising up out of the sea, having seven heads and ten horns, and on his horns ten crowns, and on his heads a blasphemous name. Now the beast which I saw was like a leopard, his feet were like the feet of a bear, and his mouth like the mouth of a lion. The dragon gave him his power, his throne, and great authority. And I saw one of his heads as if it had been mortally wounded, and his deadly wound was healed. And all the world marveled and followed the beast.
>
> (Revelation 13:1–3)

Yes, it would have elements of Medo Persia in it, the feet like a bear, and Babylon, his mouth like a lion. But it would essentially be Grecian in character and culture. In fact the head that was mortally wounded and healed is the fall of the Grecian empire and its subsequent revival at the time of the end

Daniel 8:9–14, 20–25; 9:27; 11:21–12:7; 13:1–3; Revelation 17:9–11

'Here *is* the mind which has wisdom: The seven heads are seven mountains on which the woman sits. There are also seven kings. Five have fallen, one is, *and* the other has not yet come. And when he comes, he must continue a short time. The beast that was, and is not, is himself also the eighth, and is of the seven, and is going to perdition

The seven heads are seven mountains on which the woman sitteth, and they are seven kings. The seven heads symbolise seven kingdoms which are Egypt, Assyria, Babylon, Medo Persia, Greece, Rome and the future Revised Roman empire and the beast itself is the eighth and final empire which will be Revived Greece. The entire ten kingdoms, which make seven heads will be given to the antichrist whose kingdom becomes the eighth, which the beast from the abyss helps him form and rule.

Joel 3:6 points to the fact that Greece will be the ruling power over Israel and Jerusalem at the time of the end.

> Also the people of Judah and the people of Jerusalem
> You have sold to the Greeks,
> That you may remove them far from their borders.

And Zechariah (9:13) reiterates the role of Greece at the end of days:

> For I have bent Judah, My bow,
> Fitted the bow with Ephraim,
> And raised up your sons, O Zion,
> Against your sons, O Greece,
> And made you like the sword of a mighty man.

It is this spirit of Greece who is behind all the deceiving miracles of the antichrist and his false prophet. They make even fire come down from heaven in the sight of men, give breath and power to the image of the beast to speak and do all kinds of lying wonders to deceive the people of the earth during the second half of the tribulation. That is why it is important to receive the grace of God today and be saved. God will permit the devil to do all these lying miracles. Today, if you will hear his voice, do not harden your voice.

God will have the last word over the destiny of the earth and of man when this powerful demonic prince and all his accomplices are finally captured and hurled into the lake of fire alive, where he will be tormented for ever and ever

> And I saw the beast, the kings of the earth, and their armies, gathered together to make war against Him who sat on the horse and against His army. Then the beast was captured, and with him the false prophet who worked signs in his presence, by which he deceived those who received the mark of the beast and those who worshiped his image. These two were cast alive into the lake of fire burning with brimstone.
>
> (Revelation 19:19–20)

JESUS WILL JUDGE THE NATIONS ON HIS RETURN (MATTHEW 25:31–46, 24:15–22; LUKE 21:24, ROMANS 11:25)

This judgement will take place at Jesus' Second Coming to the earth (Matthew 25:31). He will gather *all nations* before Him in the valley of Jehoshaphat (Joel 3:1–3, 2:18–20; Matthew 25:32). These are survivors of the tribulation, no more than a third of the earth's population. The single incident that will precipitate Jesus' Second Coming is 'when the power of the holy people has been completely shattered' (Daniel 12:7b). He will deliver the Jews when Israel's *enemies will overrun Jerusalem* and the *Jewish people will be on the brink of annihilation* (Zechariah 12, 13:7–9, 14:1–14). After destroying the enemies of Israel at Armageddon, He will gather all the nations and judge them (Joel 3:1–17).

The judgement will be based on how nations and individuals have treated the Jewish people during their time of dire need during the seven-year tribulation. Israel has been persecuted since they became a nation in Egypt. The time of persecution of the Jewish people is what the Bible calls the times of the Gentiles, and it is still going on today. The times of the Gentiles (Luke 21:24) refers to that period of time beginning with the history of Israel (in Egypt) to the Second Coming of Christ, during which Israel has been persecuted by the Gentiles, whether in the land or not. It means the same as the fullness of the Gentiles (Romans 11:25). It began with the oppression of Israel in Egypt and will continue through the kingdom of the Antichrist and end at the Second Coming of Christ. The fullness of the Gentiles does not refer to the salvation of a certain number of Gentiles as it is popularly believed as this would be ongoing even throughout the millennium.

The persecution of the Jewish people is going to reach its zenith during the last three and a half years of the tribulation, which the Bible calls the great tribulation or the time of Jacob's trouble (Jeremiah 30:7). For then there will be great tribulation such as has not been since the beginning of the world until this time nor ever shall be (Matthew 24:21; Mark 13:19; Luke 21:24). This is the time the Antichrist will make his final push to exterminate the Jews completely, but he will fail in his diabolical, satanic enterprise.

Throughout history, the nations that have oppressed Israel have included Egypt, Assyria (northern Iraq and southern Turkey), Babylon, Medo-Persia (Iran, Afghanistan, and Pakistan), ancient Greece (which included Turkey, Syria, and Egypt), and ancient Rome. And in the near future, it will be the *revised Roman Empire* and the *revived Greece*. So there is going to be a revision of the old Roman Empire to incorporate all the preceding ancient empires to exist for a short period and then taken over by the revised Grecian Empire (which the Antichrist will form and rule over), which will also include all the empires preceding it. I hope you are getting an idea of those nations that will form the nucleus of the Antichrist's kingdom. Just look at the nations and regions of the world quaking and shaking today. These are the very nations the Lord Jesus will fight and judge on His return.

Judgement is for (Joel 3:1–4):

1. scattering the Jews among the nations (Joel 3:2)
2. dividing up the land of Israel, especially attempting to partition Jerusalem and make East Jerusalem the capital of a future Palestinian state (Zechariah 1:14–15, 12:2–3; Ezekiel 36:5)

3. resisting the rebuilding of the desolate lands of Israel, the so-called settlements (Ezekiel 36:36, 36:1–8)
4. slandering and taunting Israel, as what happens constantly in the UN, EU, the major world powers, etc. (Ezekiel 36:3, 15)
5. swallowing Israel up on every side, without friends; in the UN, they did whatever they wished to her—slandered her, mocked her, plundered her, isolated her, ridiculed her
6. all the blasphemy against Israel and her God by the surrounding nations (Ezekiel 35:10–13; Psalm 83:4–8; etc.).

Because of constant wars and terrorism against the Jews, her young men and women are always killed (Ezekiel 36:13–14). But God says Israel would not be bereaved of her children any more. Nor hear the constant taunts of the (surrounding) nations. So yes, God will judge all nations for their treatment of Israel, especially during the seven-year tribulation. You see, God judges the Gentile nations directly, but He uses the Gentile nations to chastise or discipline the Jews. During the tribulation, the Jews will be persecuted by the whore, the great harlot of Revelation 17, then by the Antichrist and his Babylonian socio-economic political system of Revelation 18, and then by God Himself to bring them to the end of themselves so they would accept His Son, Jesus Christ. Jews would be so persecuted all over the world; be plagued with hunger, thirst, nakedness, and sickness; be as strangers, fleeing for their lives; and be put in prison (as described in Matthew 25:35–36). This is God's final judgement on Israel as His way of bringing pressure on them to turn to Him in their desperation and believe in Jesus as their long-awaited Messiah when he shows up at the end of the tribulation personally to deliver them. So the tribulation, which primarily concerns Israel, even though most of the world would be caught up in it, is an act of God's judgement and His grace at the same time (Zechariah 12:1–14, 13:6–9, 14:1–2, 12–14).

God will do this for Israel to hallow and vindicate His holy name so that Israel herself and the nations around her and the world at large will come to know that it was God who brought them back to their ancient homeland, that He was rebuilding their desolate places, the so-called settlements (Ezekiel 36:33–36). This will cause Israel to repent of their unfaithfulness to the God of their fathers and cry out to God so He will fulfil all the promises He made to their fathers, Abraham, Isaac, and Jacob (Ezekiel 36:37, 22, 32). This will bring to an end the time of the Gentiles. When Israel is restored to her land, which God gave to her fathers, it will completely change the geography of the region as we know it today as many nations will disappear.

During this time, God will be watching every nation's and every individual's treatment of Jews in their time of dire need. Jesus goes on to say that whatever anyone does for His persecuted brethren, they will be doing it for Him. 'His brethren' here refers to the *Jewish people, not the church*, because the whole context of this incident would be at His Second Coming. As Matthew 25:31 hints: 'When the Son of Man comes in His glory, and all the holy angels with Him, then He will sit on the throne of His glory.' This only happens at His second advent when He will be returning to earth, this time, with the saints who had been raptured seven years prior. This is the time He comes to sit in the throne of His glory to establish His millennial kingdom on earth and rule and reign from Jerusalem, His chosen city and the seat of His government.

Those who helped the Jews in any way (would have done it in recognition that they are God's covenant nation and must have believed in the God of Israel to be saved) are called righteous (the sheep) and be allowed to enter God's millennial kingdom. These are the natural people that would continue to live on and repopulate the earth and over whom the saints would rule and reign with Christ for a thousand years and thence into eternity.

But those nations and individuals who persecuted the Jews or refused to help them in their time of need are called cursed (goats) and sent straight, alive, to the lake of fire. These people would not appear at the great white throne judgement at the end of the millennium to be judged as they would have been judged already. These are the only class of people who go to hell alive (apart from the incident in Numbers 16:1–35). One of the main ways even *so-called* Christians will fall foul with the Lord Jesus is to support the enemies of Israel against her.

It is dangerous to be at the opposing side to God on any issue, saved or unsaved. Please take note. Unfortunately, when it comes to these crucial geopolitical issues, many people have sourced their information from the world's media. But these are mostly ignorant when it comes to these things. Hence, most people are misinformed about this conflict and have taken the wrong side at the risk of their eternal damnation.

The nations that God will punish for persecuting and oppressing Israel include:

1. Tyre and Sidon (Lebanon): Joel 3:4–8; Ezekiel 28:20–26
2. Palestine (the Gaza Strip where the Palestinians live): Joel 3:14
3. Egypt: Isaiah 19:1–22
4. Edom (Jordan): Jeremiah 49:7–8
5. Arabia (Saudi Arabia): Jeremiah 25:15–17, 23–24, 30–31, 33
6. Ethiopia (translated from Cush) southern Egypt and northern Sudan: Zephaniah 2:11–12
7. Libya: Ezekiel 30:5
8. Moab (Jordan, descendants of Lot): Zephaniah 2:8–9; Numbers 24:17
9. Ammon(Jordan, descendants of Lot): Jeremiah 25:15–30
10. Magog, Meschech, Tubal, Gomer, Togarmah, also Javan (Turkey): Ezekiel 32:26, 39:6
11. Damascus (capital of Syria): Isaiah 7:8
12. Babylonia (Iraq): Isaiah 13, 14, 49:1–6; Jeremiah 50, 51
13. Persia (Iran): Daniel 2:34–35; Revelation 13:2; Ezekiel 38:1–8
14. Assyria (southern Turkey and northern Iraq): Zechariah 10:5–12; Zephaniah 2:1–13; Micah 5:6.

These are the nations that have persecuted Israel through the years and continue to do so. It is obvious they are all Islamic nations, and they are all sworn enemies of Israel. They will be the nucleus of the beast's (the Antichrist's) empire in the very near future, which ISIS attempted to establish and failed. This is the Islamic caliphate that is currently taking shape to be headed by Turkey. They will emerge stronger and better organised next time to include all the above nations and peoples and actually capture and overrun Jerusalem (according to Zechariah 12, 13:8–9, 14:1–14; Revelation 11:2).

It will take the personal intervention of the Lord Jesus to rescue Jerusalem and the Jewish people from total annihilation. On Jesus' return to earth, there will be a fierce battle raging in Jerusalem, and half of the city would have fallen to the Antichrist and his invading forces, so His first priority would be the liberation of Jerusalem and saving the Jewish people from extermination. Unfortunately, this is a family feud started in the tents of Abraham (Genesis 21:8–14) and has gone global to suck virtually the whole world in. It is Abraham's descendants disputing over the family inheritance, and it will take another descendant of Abraham, the Lord Jesus, to come and settle the dispute.

The world has never understood the root causes of this conflict, hence their inability to resolve it. This ancient family feud has morphed into a dispute for Palestinian statehood, but the Palestinians had never been a nation and never a homogeneous people until a couple of decades ago when that was concocted as the pretext for Arab–Muslim dissatisfaction. Let us pray for both sides of the conflict because it affects us all, and the bottom line is that God loves all people and wants all to come and know Him and be saved through His Son, Jesus.

It does not mean these are the only nations God will judge on His return, but these will be His main focus. He will judge all nations for their part in persecuting Israel, especially through the UN, EU, national governments, and parastate organisations. God will also judge nations for rejecting His offer of salvation through the sacrifice of His Son, Jesus, and for their rebellion and sin.

HELL'S HALL OF FAME

God has reserved a special place in the depths of hell for those who have practised terrorism on the earth. He will group them according to their country of origin for special punishment. In Ezekiel 32:17–32, these are clearly listed.

I will give highlights of these here:

> 'Son of man, wail over the multitude of Egypt,
> And cast them down to the depths of the earth,
> Her and the daughters of the famous nations,
> With those who go down to the Pit.
>
> (Ezekiel 32:18)

This has reference to terrorists from Iraq and Syria:

> 'Assyria is there, and all her company,
> With their graves all around her,
> All of them slain, fallen by the sword.
> ²³ Her graves are set in the recesses of the Pit,
> And her company is all around her grave,
> All of them slain, fallen by the sword,
> Who caused terror in the land of the living.
>
> (Ezekiel 32:22–23)

This has reference to terrorists from Saudi Arabia:

> 'There is Elam and all her multitude,
> All around her grave,
> All of them slain, fallen by the sword,
> Who have gone down uncircumcised to the lower parts
> of the earth,
> Who caused their terror in the land of the living;
> Now they bear their shame with those who go down
> to the Pit.
>
> (Ezekiel 32:24)

These have reference to terrorists from Turkey:

> 'There are Meshech and Tubal and all their multitudes,
> With all their graves around it,

All of them uncircumcised, slain by the sword,
Though they caused their terror in the land of the living.

(Ezekiel 32:26)

This has reference to Palestinians and Jordanians:

There is Edom,
Her kings and all her princes,
Who despite their might
Are laid beside those slain by the sword;
They shall lie with the uncircumcised,
And with those who go down to the Pit.

(Ezekiel 32:29)

This has reference to Syrians and Lebanese, especially Hezbollah:

There are the princes of the north,
All of them, and all the Sidonians,
Who have gone down with the slain
In shame at the terror which they caused by their might;
They lie uncircumcised with those slain by the sword,
And bear their shame with those who go down to the Pit.

(Ezekiel 32:30)

This could have reference to Egypt, but it also refers to the Antichrist and his followers, who will massacre multitudes of Jews and tribulation saints:

'Pharaoh will see them
And be comforted over all his multitude,
Pharaoh and all his army,
Slain by the sword,'
Says the Lord GOD.
[32] 'For I have caused My terror in the land of the living;
And he shall be placed in the midst of the uncircumcised

With those slain by the sword,
Pharaoh and all his multitude,'
Says the Lord GOD.

(Ezekiel 32:31–32)

It is obvious God has not listed all terrorist nations and regions, but He is serving notice that nothing escapes His attention.

GET TO KNOW JESUS WHILE THERE IS STILL TIME

Going to heaven has nothing to do with being a good person; it is about knowing the person of Jesus Christ as your Lord and Saviour by accepting His redemptive work on the cross for you. Today, if you will hear His voice, do not harden your hearts (Psalm 95:8). Tomorrow may be too late.

You can accept Jesus as your Lord and Saviour by saying this simple prayer and by believing in Him in your heart: 'Lord Jesus, I acknowledge that I am a sinner. I believe you are the Son of God and that you died on the cross for my sins. I now invite you into my heart to be my Lord and saviour. Thank you for Saving my soul. Amen' (Romans 10:9–11, 13).

After saying this prayer, you are born again. You need to find a church which will teach you the Word of God so you can grow in your new faith.

You may be saying, 'Well, I am not sure I'm ready to say that prayer just yet. I need more information.' I will encourage you to pray and ask God to reveal the truth about Jesus to you. Say, 'God, I want to know if Jesus is Your Son, if it is true that He died and rose again from the dead, and if He is God and the Saviour of mankind as Christians believe and as the Bible teaches. And if all these are true about Jesus, I would like Him to be my Lord and Saviour as well.'

Unfortunately, the testimony of scripture is clear. Many *professing Christians* will find themselves *in hell* to their utter shock and consternation. Please check all these scriptures and examine yourself before it is too late: Matthew 7:21–23; Matthew 25:1–13, 14–30; Luke 10:25–27, 13:22–27; 1 Corinthians 10:1–12; Romans 11:21–22.

Are you a Christian? Then be assured of your salvation. Go on to develop an intimate relationship with the Lord. It is all about getting to know Jesus through spending time with Him in the Word of God and through prayer. Remember, God *will not admit any stranger* into His heavenly abode. Make sure you confess and repent of all known sins. Don't ignore the destructive power of sin. It could wreck your eternal destiny, so don't play with sin or entertain it in any shape or form in your life. Yes, God does not demand perfection from any of us because it is unattainable on this side of eternity. But that is not the same as ignoring known sin to fester in your life.

Second Corinthians 13:5 says, 'Examine yourself as to whether you are in the faith. Test yourselves. Do you not know yourselves, that Jesus Christ is in you?—unless indeed you are disqualified.'

John 20:30–31 states: 'And many other signs truly did Jesus in the presence of his disciples, which are not written in this book: 31 But these are written, that ye might believe that Jesus is the Christ, the Son of God; and that believing ye might have life through his name.'

Believe the testimony of scripture which says if you have believed in Him, then you have eternal life in His name. You do not have to look different or feel different, but the Bible says you become different.

> These things I have written to you who believe in the
> name of the Son of God, that you may know that you
> have eternal life.
>
> (1 John 5:13)

The beauty of biblical Christianity is that if you are saved, you have the assurance in your heart. You know whether your sins are forgiven or not. You don't wait to die to find out, by which time it might be all too late. Halleluiah! Glory to God. Do a periodic self-evaluation of your walk with the Lord. Ask Him to show you areas in your life you need to work on, and by His Grace, I'll see you in heaven. Amen.